RIVERS
of
GOLD

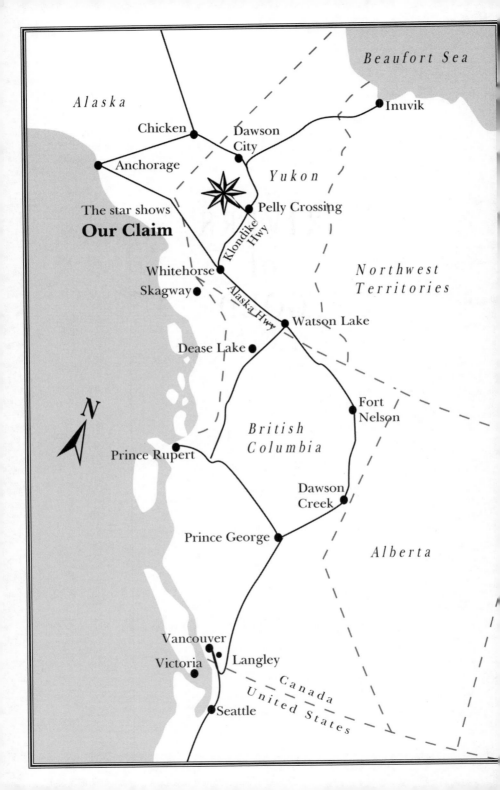

RIVERS
of
GOLD

A True Yukon Story

BY

GWEN & DON LEE

hancock

house

ISBN 0-88839-555-8

Cataloging in Publication Data

Lee, Gwen, 1930-
　　Rivers of gold : a true Yukon story / by Gwen & Don Lee.

ISBN 0-88839-555-8

　　1. Lee, Don, 1926- 2. Lee, Gwen, 1930- 3. Gold miners--Yukon
Territory--Biography. 4. Prospecting--Yukon Territory. 5. Yukon
Territory--Biography. I. Lee, Don, 1926- II. Title.

TN140.L435A3 2004　　　622'.3422'09227191　　　C2004-902220-2

Printed in China—JADE

Published simultaneously in Canada and the United States by

HANCOCK HOUSE PUBLISHERS LTD.
19313 Zero Avenue, Surrey, B.C. V3S 9R9
(604) 538-1114 Fax (604) 538-2262

HANCOCK HOUSE PUBLISHERS
1431 Harrison Avenue, Blaine, WA 98230-5005
(604) 538-1114 Fax (604) 538-2262
Web Site: www.hancockhouse.com *email:* sales@hancockhouse.com

Table of Contents

Dedicated

to our children

and

grandchildren,

with love.

About the Authors

Don Lee was born in Westlock, Alberta, in 1926, the oldest of five children in a farming family. His mother, of German descent, and his father, of Norwegian/Icelandic descent, were from pioneering stock. They put many backbreaking years into developing two sections of farmland in northern Alberta, cultivating the land at first with teams of horses. Almost every type of animal was raised on this farm – pigs, chickens, turkeys, cows and horses – and the family also bred silver foxes for their pelts. Don's parents grew a large vegetable garden every summer and visitors never went away empty-handed. Don worked hard on the farm from a young age and learned to love and respect the outdoor life. He also ran a trapline as a youth.

Gwen Roberts was born in 1930 in Edmonton, Alberta, second daughter of a family that settled in Langley, B.C. in 1932. She was named Tegwen by her Welsh father and her English mother. When the family arrived in the Fraser Valley, Langley was a rural agricultural community. Gwen, the second of four children, grew up in a happy household where both parents doted on the children but also provided very definite role models when it came to outdoor and indoor chores. Anything outside was Dad's job, and the indoor housework, cooking and sewing was Mom's job. How different a life Gwen would have after she married Don!

When Don's family sold the farm and moved to British Columbia in 1945, Don, as a nineteen-year-old, got a job in heavy construction, a field that would involve him for the next twenty years.

In 1948 Don and Gwen met; they married the same year. A son, Brian, was born the year after they were married, and shortly after that the treks to remote construction sites that would extend over the next seventeen years began. Whenever possible, the family moved to the job location. In 1957 a daughter, Linda, was born.

Work on large earth-moving schemes such as dams and power

projects, as well as the St. Lawrence Seaway, took the family across Canada and into the Yukon. At a Mayo, Yukon dam project in the early 1950s Don started to think about the famed Yukon gold strikes. In his spare time he built a small sluice-box. He ran the gravel at the job site through it and began to brag about having seen his first "colours" – flecks of gold. This earned him the nickname, "Sluice-box Kid."

The construction jobs Don was involved in required excavation of tremendous volumes of earth and the use of a wide variety of heavy equipment. He gained skills he would find invaluable in gold mining. Don learned how to operate each machine and rose first to foreman, then general foreman and then superintendent over various phases of earth and rock digging, moving, replacing and building.

His construction work gradually increased his knowledge of soil, rocks and minerals. It was on a job in the Bridge River area of B.C. that Don stumbled upon his first boulder of jade, which at this time was thought to be alluvial and found only in creeks. Jade became Don's fascination and it was later to become his "green gold." Finding the jade boulder turned him into a rockhound. He traded part of it to Ross Tanner, who knew how to cut opals, having learned it from an old European artisan. Ross would show Don and Gwen how to cut and polish stones. The Lees were enthralled to see the colours winking and blinking as the opal was rotated.

Years of intensive study of jade led to the Lees' staking claims in the Bridge River area. They joined Bob Smith of Greenbay Mining in establishing a world market for jade. Don's experience with jade over the years has made him one of the most knowledgable people on the subject in British Columbia. Jade mining also rekindled Don's dream of a gold mine.

Except for the time spent at construction jobs from Vancouver Island to Quebec, Langley has continued to be home for the Lees. It is the place Gwen and Don chose in 1965 as the location of their own rock shop, specializing in jade and opals, and it has been the base for all their other ventures in B.C. and the Yukon. Whether they are finding and marketing precious stones, retailing jewellery and giftware, doing gardening or mining for gold, they always work as a team.

Preface

Dawson City, now a restored historic site, originally sprang to life back in 1896 with the onset of the Klondike Gold Rush. The town's historical records say that in Rabbit Creek (now known as Bonanza Creek), Dawson Charlie, George Carmacks and Skookum Jim made the first major find of gold nuggets. After two tons of gold from the creeks flowing into the Klondike River arrived in Seattle, word quickly travelled around the world. The stampede north began.

By 1898 Dawson, snuggled against the hills at the confluence of the Klondike and Yukon Rivers, had become the hub of the gold rush and, at 30,000 population, was the largest city north of San Francisco and west of Winnipeg. It had telephone service, steam heat and running water. Elaborate dance halls, theatres and hotels were erected and Dawson City was called by some, "Paris of the North." One year later the stampede was over. Eight thousand people left Dawson during the summer of 1899, and by 1902 the city's population had shrunk to less than 5,000. . . .

In the summer of 1998, one hundred years after the Klondike Gold Rush, the tourist season had arrived in Dawson. The town's normal population of 2,000 was swollen with some of the 30,000 visitors that crowd the streets each year. They had come from all corners of the earth to see this famous town with its unpaved streets, board sidewalks and unique restored century-old buildings.

A gusty breeze caught the wind chimes hanging on the verandah of our Rivers of Gold gift shop. They swung to their full length, loudly and persistently announcing a swiftly arriving storm. The fluffy white clouds that had so recently decorated the sky had merged and taken on a dark hue. Now, on this late afternoon in July, they rolled threateningly above Dawson City.

Suddenly the sky was split by jagged lines of lightning, followed by a deafening clap of thunder. Immediately the heavens opened, sending a cloudburst of rain that ricocheted off the ground and the board-walks. This sent everyone scurrying for cover.

The open door of Rivers of Gold Gift Shop was an inviting refuge for some of the tourists who had been casually strolling the streets moments before. An elderly couple were the first inside. The petite, grey-haired lady asked, "Could we wait in your store until the rain stops – or at least lessens?"

"Of course," I replied.

"This really caught us unawares. Do you often get changeable weather like this?" the lady inquired.

"Yes, it is quite common for us to have sunshine, rain, wind and then sunshine again, all within an hour or so," I answered. "Just wait, you may soon see a beautiful rainbow."

"As you can see," she explained, "we were prepared for only warm weather."

Their scanty, lightweight tops and shorts affirmed this statement. Introductions ensued, and I learned that Betty and Jack were visiting from California. Soon several other tourists who'd entered the store joined our conversation.

"Do you live here?" asked one.

"No," I explained, "but I am no stranger to the Yukon. I've been in and out of the Territory since 1951. Jewellery and giftware are my main loves, but my husband has always been an outdoor enthusiast, with a fascination for mining. We had a gold mine in this Dawson mining area. There are some pictures on the back wall, if any of you would like to see how we mined for gold."

Immediately a question arose: "Do you still have the mine?"

"No," I responded. "It's a long story. These pictures on the wall bring back many, many memories – some good, some sad. But it was a tremendous experience."

It was the ensuing question, "How did you get started?" that brought the memories to life in my mind.

The storm had now picked up momentum. The wind chimes were clanging loudly. It was as if they were calling for attention because they knew I was about to begin my story. . . .

CHAPTER 1

The Lure of Yukon Gold

The words "gold" and "mining" when used together carry a deep fascination for man. My husband Don and I were no different. For some, these two words conjure up images of riches, power, fame and luck, not to mention feelings of euphoria. For others the words connote hardship, greed, evil and poverty.

In reality, there were a few who did strike it rich in the Klondike Gold Rush of 1898 in Canada's northern lands, but there were many more who lost everything. Instead of extracting from Mother Nature, they added what little they had to the famed Klondike. The saying, "There's gold in them thar hills," is true. Many people helped put it there, and Don and I are among them.

Our small family, living in Langley, British Columbia, in the heart of the Fraser Valley, decided to try its luck at gold mining. The hunt for gold began in 1976 when Don, the family head, decided in his Napoleonic fashion that placer mining would be a fascinating thing to do. We were already in jade mining, but in Don's mind, gold mining would be a challenge – and Don loved challenges. Therefore, we must get a gold mine.

Don began educating himself on the subject. He obtained the complete set of B.C. hardcover mining books – called "Report of the Minister of Mines" – put out annually from 1905 to 1969. For over two years he studied, read and reread these books and maps, in anticipation of finding the perfect place to stake a gold mine. He became intensely interested in the Cassiar area of northwestern B.C., especially because there was a probability of finding jade in the area, along with gold. His decision made, planning was under way to stake claims in this region.

At the same time, British Columbia was in the midst of an election. The outcome was a New Democratic Party (NDP) victory. This

Map not to scale

temporarily squelched the mining plans, for the NDP government was not encouraging to mining. In fact, they made it extremely difficult.

A short while later, a friend and customer very knowledgable in mining, Ken Christie, came into the shop and asked how the mining plans were going. Don explained that he'd had to forget about them, due to the information he'd received regarding the B.C. government's blocks to new exploration.

"Why don't you go to the Yukon?" suggested Ken.

The wheels began turning once again in Don's head. He began focusing his studies on the section of Canada situated north of the province of B.C., known officially as Yukon Territory. In particular, he investigated Scroggie Creek and Barker Creek, where nearly all the work had been done by hand. No powered machinery, which greatly increased the amount of gravel that could be mined, had ever been used.

In the year 1978 Don turned fifty-two and I was now forty-eight. We had been working steadily for years and had not taken a vacation for a very long time. Lee's Jade and Opals, our shop in Langley, was doing well and we decided it was high time we took a holiday. Funny thing was, when it came time to decide what we most enjoyed doing, we realized that the majority of our hobbies and pleasures were work-related. Well, Don still had his head wrapped around the idea of gold mining, so it didn't take him long to suggest this connection to our holiday. I certainly wasn't opposed to the idea – it sounded exciting.

By August our plans were finalized. We would travel to Dawson City, spend some leisurely time there, then stake mining leases at Scroggie and Barker Creeks respectively.

CHAPTER 2

Staking Our Claims

It wasn't a vacation in the tropics, but we decided that a couple could go on a holiday such as Club Med for $1000 each, and this established what we would spend. In August 1978 we fitted out the back of our Ford three-quarter-ton pickup truck with a bed and foamies for a mattress. We packed a Coleman camp stove, dishes, cooking utensils and a few plastic pails and bowls; cooler chests held the groceries and thus we were for the most part self-sufficient. We could heat up water for coffee breaks, dishwashing and sponge baths. What more could we possibly ask for? We were Yukon-bound!

Our travelling was made smooth thanks to cooperative weather, plus extensive route knowledge gained during our commutes to the Yukon when Don worked there in 1951. Also, highway conditions had greatly improved since that time. Having previously driven both routes to the Yukon, we chose the shortest one, west from Prince George on Highway 16 then north on the Cassiar Highway to where it meets the Alaska Highway near Watson Lake in the Yukon Territory. The alternative route goes through Dawson Creek and onto the Alaska Highway.

The hills were already sporting golden splashes of colour that intermingled beautifully with the many shades of green. The absence of buildings for miles at a time created a sense of isolation and a special peaceful quietness.

On arriving in Whitehorse, we decided to stop for a full, hearty breakfast at one of the hotels. We bumped into two people we had known well years ago in Langley – former neighbours of Don's parents. Ed Isaac and his sister, Lila, both very musical, had been hired to entertain at the hotel. So our breakfast turned into an hour of getting caught up on years of family happenings.

Beyond Whitehorse, we headed north again on the Klondike

Highway and were pleasantly surprised to find that both Pelly Crossing and Stewart Crossing had new bridges. In the 1950s we had made the crossing either by ferry (in summer, and when the ice was thin enough for the ferry to go through it), or by the ice bridge (when the ice was thick enough to drive over it). Those wanting to travel during times when the ice wasn't thin or thick enough were – you guessed it – just plain out of luck! You can see why we were "happy campers" when we came upon an authentic bridge.

This time we were travelling on to Dawson instead of veering off east for Mayo, so from the intersection with Highway 11, this was new territory for us. We continued following the Klondike Highway until a few houses and buildings came into view. We assumed this was a small settlement outside of Dawson City. Then, viewing the river on one side and several buildings on the other, we were astounded to discover that this, in fact, was all that was left of the famous town from the Klondike Gold Rush. What had once been the biggest city north of San Francisco had been reduced to what we were seeing on Front Street.

At this point we checked out of the "Lee Hotel" (our truck) and into the Eldorado Hotel – our first and only legitimate hotel of the entire vacation. We adjusted to being ordinary sightseers for a few days. It was a small yet captivating city. We especially enjoyed touring the wonderful museum and visiting Diamond Tooth Gertie's gambling hall, bar and can-can show. In 1978, Diamond Tooth Gertie's was the only casino in Canada with legalized gambling. Another highlight for us was the fascinating musical presentation called "Gaslight Follies" at the Palace Grand. This particular performance was never quite surpassed in any of our future visits.

After completing our exploration of Dawson, we were ready to embark on the next segment of our adventure – staking gold leases. From our temporary headquarters at the Eldorado Hotel, we made reservations with Trans North for a helicopter to take us to the two areas we had plotted on the map. Early the next morning we met Rod Watt, a pleasant young helicopter pilot, and without much ado we lifted off for our first destination, Scroggie Creek.

It took us approximately fifty minutes of flying over hills, valleys, forest and muskeg to arrive at Scroggie Creek, which is three

Aerial view of Dawson City—where the Klondike River enters the Yukon Rive

Don at old cabin at the Scroggie Creek claim.

degrees below the Arctic Circle. We were delighted to discover that, only three miles from this lease, there was an old runway, built and used during World War II, sufficient for landing a small fixed-wing craft. This would be of great assistance for bringing in supplies in the future.

We were pleased with all that we observed at this site. We found a cute little log cabin which, with a little work, we knew we could make quite habitable. We were also intrigued to come across some old diggings and tunnelling. The aged picks and shovels that had been used for this were still leaning against the cribbing. The whole atmosphere was inspiring to us. With growing anticipation of our future here, we staked and named our lease. It became the "Four Niner", after the four nines that had appeared on our truck's odometer as we were entering the city of Dawson.

We returned to the helicopter, and after a short flight we arrived at Barker Creek, our final destination. Landing was definitely more of a problem here, as small brush was growing up everywhere. Once that was accomplished, Rod began testing the ground to ensure the chopper wouldn't sink into the muskeg, and Don and I began our exploration. Somehow it seemed more isolated here. Perhaps this was because of the surrounding hills that closed in on us and limited our vision. In spite of this, it didn't take us long to stake our lease and determine its name, after glancing above to see the most beautiful rainbow draw itself across the sky. What could be more indicative of prosperity than the symbolic pot of gold that's to be found at the end of each rainbow?

"Rainbow", as we named this lease, also showed evidence of hard work, tunnelling and test holes. As far as we could determine, though, no machine had been on this property. With that in mind we believed it would be a good one to work. It too had remnants of an old cabin. Unfortunately, this one was very much in disrepair and beyond saving. Judging by the contents left behind, we presumed a family must have lived here in the past. We discovered old bottles, a lamp, a dish, a doll with a missing arm and a tattered issue of Life magazine from 1937. We picked up the old magazine and the tiny glass dish for souvenirs from the staking of our Barker Creek lease, and headed back to Dawson.

Our staking completed and our leases recorded in the Dawson mining office, we now headed for home. We marvelled at the panoramic views of fall colours and photographed some of the more scenic spots.

The roads south of Dawson were dusty and rough, but we still managed to make good time. Don bragged that we hadn't had a flat tire. That day we got not one, but two flats within 30 miles! Fortunately we were carrying two spares. We only lost the time it took to get them repaired in Carmacks, further down the Klondike Highway. The culprit in both cases was steel shavings off the road-grader's blade.

CHAPTER 3

Six Months of Planning

Once back home, the realization of what we had done, and the commitment it was going to require from us in the future, seemed to finally hit us. We couldn't quite believe it. To begin with, it meant a trip to the Yukon to do the required assessment work for the Barker Creek and Scroggie Creek leases the following year. It meant gathering information on weather, terrain, property owners and registered traplines. It also meant putting a great amount of consideration into the equipment we would need, not only to make the trip, but also to start mining. All things considered, we realized we had to begin our planning right away!

The trip would have to be made in winter. There were no roads to either the Scroggie or Barker Creek property, so in the summer it was impossible to get people or supplies there and back except by helicopter or airplane. Helicopters at $600 per trip were an expense we wanted to avoid whenever possible. During the summer working season, Dawson with its aircraft-rental firms was going to be our hub. In the winter, however, we could leave the highway at Pelly Crossing and travel by bulldozer across the snow. We would take the heavy equipment and as many supplies as possible to our leases during this season. Machinery could be taken in only when the ground was frozen because environmental damage would be caused in the swampy muskeg at any other time. Besides, machines such as bulldozers and front-end loaders were too heavy to fly in, therefore winter trips were a necessity.

In an issue of National Geographic we happened upon an article concerning Pelly Ranch, owned by the Bradleys. The ranch was approximately 30 miles from Pelly Crossing. From this point we could head through the bush to our mining property at Scroggie Creek. For this reason, we thought it would be a great idea to write a letter to the Bradleys, introduce ourselves, and tell them of our proposed trip. In the letter we explained that we had decided to bring our supplies through in March.

We were pleased to receive a prompt reply from Marjorie Bradley. She let us know that she, her husband Dick and his brother Hugh, all co-owners of the ranch, would love for us to stop at the ranch as we passed by. She was also kind enough to give us the name of Peter Isaac, who had a registered trapline in the area through which we'd be travelling, so that we could write to him.

We were informed that in late March there would be approximately 18 inches of snow in the area. Don decided that he would require a small bulldozer for the ground testing and work. A bulldozer would also be capable of pulling a trailer load of fuel and supplies. Don constructed what he thought would be an ideal heavy rubber-tired trailer, and the end of the search for a reasonably priced bulldozer came when he chose a John Deere model 450B machine. It was equipped with a winch, and ice lugs were welded to the tracks as there would be small glaciers and icy sections on the route. The winch would prove to be a lifesaver.

Our family made a unanimous decision that this first winter trip would be made by Don and our son-in-law, Forrest. I was to be spared this trip. Don was accustomed to the bush, had a trapline as a teenager in Northern Alberta, and had already spent two March months in the Yukon, so he was confident there would be nothing they couldn't handle. For my peace of mind, we made arrangements with Trans North that any time a helicopter was flying in the area the men were travelling, the pilot would keep an eye out for them. After returning, he would call me

Rubber tired trailer and John Deere bulldozer—our work horses

Getting the first load for the Yukon ready to go.

Rivers of Gold

or my daughter, Linda, and give us a report on our husbands' progress.

The men wisely resolved to haul along a snowmobile for each of them in case they broke down and became stranded. This would also enable them to make the return trip from Scroggie Creek on land. Forrest was covered – he already owned an Arctic Cat Pantera. Don was not. Trying, as always, to save on costs, Don looked into renting a snowmobile. That idea was scrapped quickly when we learned that renting one was actually more expensive than buying one. We were soon the owners of a brand-new Arctic Cat Panther! These would be loaded onto Don's lowbed, and Forrest's Peterbilt tractor truck would get the load to Pelly Crossing.

As the time of their departure got closer, the planning was becoming more detailed. For example, what would they eat? After all, fresh fruits, canned foods, and almost everything we could think of would freeze in that cold weather. We realized that almost everything would have to be dehydrated foods. We selected freeze-dried packages that mountain climbers use, making sure to include ones that would sustain their protein needs, for example pork chops.

To balance the meals as much as we could, we also included instant mashed potatoes, dehydrated mixed vegetables, five-minute rice, Sapporo instant soups and dried fruit. We threw in raisins and chocolates for times when they would need a quick energy boost and had no time to stop and cook. We even designed it so their meals could be cooked and eaten as quickly and easily as possible. Put the water in the pot, add the dried meat, next the dehydrated vegetables and top the pot off at the end with the instant potatoes or five-minute rice. In theory it sounded perfect. They were going to eat quickly-made, well-balanced meals.

The only thing left to do was load all the supplies. At this point our yard in Langley became a hub of activity. The size of the trailer limited the amount of goods we could transport. Already we had loaded ten barrels of fuel plus oil, grease, water pumps, a small sluice-box, hoses, tents, tarps, two five-star down-filled sleeping bags that cost $800 each, tools, various other camp supplies and all that delicious food. This fully burdened trailer then had to be loaded onto the lowbed, alongside the John Deere caterpillar and the two snowmobiles. What a busy day that was!

With everything loaded, Don and Forrest were ready for the road. The trip was scheduled so that after everything was accomplished, we'd have them home safe and sound in approximately fourteen days. It would take them three days to travel from Langley to Pelly Crossing and unload, a week to get from there to Scroggie Creek, one day to come out by snowmobile and three days back to Langley.

It looked flawless on paper. We forgot just one thing – Murphy's Law!

CHAPTER 4

Reality Check–
The First Winter Trip

Don and Forrest's March 1979 trip began just as ideally as it was organized. From Langley to Pelly Crossing all went well – winter road conditions were as anticipated and they reached Pelly Crossing on schedule. However, uneasiness first began when they noticed light rain falling as they came to Pelly Crossing.

"Forrest, do you think we're going to have enough snow, or could this be early break-up?" Don mentioned with sudden concern.

"We'd better!" exclaimed Forrest. Only later would they be able to look back at the ludicrous irony of their worry over not having enough snow!

They unloaded everything and made arrangements to leave the truck in the care of the nearby First Nations village until their return. Don and Forrest made camp for the night and put their outdoor-freezing-weather culinary abilities to the test. They brought out the eggs, their only source of fresh food, to find that they had frozen solid. Don figured that they would have made great cannon balls, but, as these were not required at the time, they had to resign themselves to tossing them out. With only a tarp between them and the open skies, the men crept into their sleeping bags, thankful that the rain had stopped.

Morning dawned cloudy and overcast, so they decided there wasn't time to indulge themselves with much food. Don and Forrest made a hasty breakfast over a campfire and got under way as quickly as possible. The bulldozer, their mode of transportation for this stage, pulled the trailer – at approximately three and a half miles an hour – along the sparsely used road to Pelly Ranch. They were getting further and further away from civilization. Don and Forrest reached the edge of Pelly Ranch just as darkness came upon them, so they decided to make camp.

They awoke the following morning to find that the weather had changed considerably overnight. It was now much colder, and a heavy frost had spread across the ground. Once again, breakfast was made in haste and they quickly packed up in order to get back onto the trail that skirted Pelly Ranch.

Just as they were about to leave they noticed an old red tractor chugging across the open field. It was Pelly Ranch owners Hugh and Dick Bradley. The first meeting Don and Forrest had with the Bradleys included a proper scolding for staying outdoors overnight instead of coming into the ranch house. As it is termed in these parts, Don and Forrest received "old billy o' heck"!

It was a wonderful introduction to the true northern hospitality we would all come to know. Hugh and Dick proceeded to give Don and Forrest lots of helpful advice, and before heading on their way they were invited to stop at the ranch on their return from Scroggie. After a willing and enthusiastic promise to call in on the way back, Don and Forrest were on their way again.

They covered the next two to three miles relatively easily until they came to Farm Creek – the one the Bradleys had warned them about. Their guess that it might create difficulty was validated! Water was running over the frozen ice, freezing and widening, and creating a sheet of ice in the valley bottom. Up to this point Don and Forrest had been trying to follow the old stagecoach trail. However, it became a challenge at times deciding how to do this, due to years of weather damage, slides, falling trees and washouts. Should they stay on the trail, go in the creek, or continue somewhere in between? Each step of the way seemed to require a similar decision.

The two men took turns driving the John Deere and either walking, or riding on the load. The continuously flowing water froze into ice, creating a glacier. Even the ice lugs welded to the tracks could not stop the caterpillar from sliding across the frozen surface. Then suddenly – whoops! – they broke through the ice. Luckily it was only two feet deep. Once out of the creek, their attempts at widening the road were another matter.

"Damn it!" fumed Don, as he realized that they had not only damaged, but broken, the sidearm that attached the blade to the C-frame. The two men proceeded to let out a string of profanities while looking at one another helplessly. They absolutely needed the blade in order to help break trail. They had to decide whether to go back to the ranch and get help to fix it, or try to do a temporary repair themselves. Not surprisingly, they made the latter decision, and with a chain and a cinch a "haywire" repair job was done. By the end of this job they were really wishing they had brought along hip waders – but who would have thought to pack rubber boots for a Yukon winter trip?

The journey resumed and they slogged on, finally able to leave the creek bottom and get onto higher ground. This lasted for only a few miles before they dropped down into another valley. It was already time to quit for the day, and they had completed less than half of their expected distance. It was disheartening. To make matters worse, the snow was getting much deeper, setting the stage for further problems.

"Sure wish we'd put the skis on the trailer, Forrest," Don ruminated. Before they left he had wanted to make metal skis for the tires to fit in. He was, unfortunately, overruled when it was pointed out that there was supposed to be only 18 inches of snow. By now the expected 18 inches had already turned into three-plus feet!

"Ready for the menu, Dad?" quipped Forrest, knowing it would be a one-pot supper, painfully cooked over a smoky campfire with icy-cold hands barely able to hold onto the utensils. What fun! Fine twigs from the spruce trees were used to begin the fire and gradually bigger pieces were added. Often, to make tea, they melted snow in a tin pail that they hung over the fire on a green stick jammed into the snow. At one point Forrest wondered, "Dad, do you think we ever get rabbit turds in the tea?"

"Well, the leftovers in the pail are either tea leaves, spruce needles or rabbit droppings," replied Don. In this cold, a hot drink was so welcoming that somehow, even with this disturbing speculation, they were not turned off the next round of tea. The day ended with them climbing into their sleeping bags fully clothed, dirty and very tired.

Morning began with the familiar ritual of a drink of tea and something quick to eat in preparation for the day. Problems presented themselves immediately. The snow became so deep that Don and Forrest had to drop the trailer, bulldoze a path about a half mile long, go back and pick up the trailer, and then travel the half mile they had cleared. This pattern was far from a one-time occurrence; in fact, it became the procedure they had to follow for days to come.

They decided to do not more than a half mile so that the supply trailer would not be too far behind if there was ever a machinery breakdown. With the luck they'd had so far, they were beginning to believe anything could happen. Their fourteen-day plan was shot already, and it was only getting worse. For each half mile they advanced, one and a half miles of travel was required. Of course, far more fuel was being used than they had anticipated. Could things get much worse? They could and they would.

Not long after, Don and Forrest awoke from another cold night under the stars to discover, to their dismay, that the bulldozer would not start. As usual, they had shut it off the night before, not realizing that the unforeseen drop in temperature overnight to -30°F would incapacitate it. To make matters even worse, they only had summer diesel with them. They hadn't anticipated that mid-March weather could get so cold.

"Only one thing we can do," said Don. "Fill that washtub with snow, bring it to boiling, and then pour it over the fuel line, tank and motor to get the fuel to flow."

They lit a big fire that would also warm the area around the John Deere and then went ahead with Don's suggestion. By this time both men's tempers were testy, yet somehow they managed to continue talking to one another and coping with each oncoming problem.

The strategy worked, and the machine started. Neither of them were presuming this luck would last, however. After all, obstacles were becoming an expected component of their trip. The only element of surprise was what the next one would be.

It was now time to attend to their own damages. "Damn, but my lips are sore," complained Don. "I see yours are also cracked, Forrest. What's in the first-aid kit that will help?"

Forrest began pulling the first-aid supplies out one by one, but found nothing for chapped lips. "Dad, this is the only thing that may work," he finally announced, holding up a tube of Preparation H. Unthinkable as it may be, it did work! I wonder what the manufacturers of Preparation H would think about the fact that their product eases the cracking and bleeding of lips. Perhaps here's a new selling angle they could promote!

The two men were always on the lookout for flowing water. It was important not only for cooking and making their tea, but for washing. Flowing water occurs when the creek freezes to the bottom but water still flows from its source. It can't go in the natural channel, so it goes over the top. Another water source can be found in some creeks that are deep enough that the water continues flowing under the ice. It can be obtained by chopping a hole in the ice. Don and Forrest used these two methods of gathering water whenever possible.

Supplying the men's water needs was the beneficial side of the water overflow situation. On the other hand, as at Farm Creek the overflows spread and froze, becoming growing glaciers during the winter months. Always on a downhill grade, they could not be avoided because they crossed the trail to Scroggie. Tense and hair-raising moments arose in many instances when it was necessary to travel uphill over the glaciers. At times the men would find the bulldozer winding side to side or sliding backwards. In these situations, they had to try to change angles to continue fighting their way forward. Many times, treacherous spots necessitated unhitching the trailer, going on with the bulldozer alone, backing up against a tree that was sticking up through the ice, and winching the trailer up.

It was imperative in these situations that they find somewhere to anchor the trailer whenever it had to be unhitched. Without this precaution the trailer was in danger of sailing backwards over the ice, and in all probability, upsetting. This whole procedure, when it occurred, took a toll on the men's spirits as well as their bodies. It was slow, tiring and often extremely discouraging work, especially when it looked like this pace of travel was not going to end anytime soon. The stagecoach trail that they had been trying to follow was winding uphill to higher ground. It was going to be the same old story for some time to come.

Around this time Forrest, wishfully thinking, declared, "I think that's Scroggie just ahead." Of course it was days away yet, but hope was about the only thing that was keeping Don and Forrest going now. Hearty meals certainly weren't. It wasn't for lack of food – there was plenty of that left. It was only time and the energy to eat that they were lacking. Survival eating was all they could manage now. They took an occasional break, just long enough to wolf down a quick hand-to-mouth meal, and then they were off again.

They continued, ploughing through three-foot-deep snow, until they saw a ridge of trees in the distance. The trees continued to thicken as they neared the creek bottom. When they eventually arrived, they came upon remnants of old cabins. They were made of logs, approximately six to eight inches in diameter, the average size of the trees that grew in the draw.

Don and Forrest decided to take a break here and poke around. One of the cabins still had a roof; this had probably been a trapper's cabin. The others were roofless, their walls leaning in drunken fashion, remnants of a time gone by. Likely the group of cabins were those remaining from a stagecoach stopover used to house people and horses.

Could those old logs have talked, what stories they could tell of days long past! Stories of miners, dance-hall girls and many others who were heading for Dawson City with visions of fame, fortune and gold. It was at stopovers like this that both horses and people would have been fed and given a well-earned rest. The horses would have been changed, and the replacement team of horsepower would be hitched to the stagecoach when the journey resumed. I can only imagine what hardships people must have endured on that trail back in 1898. Eighty years later, Don and Forrest were experiencing the cold and other adversities of this lonely land. In fact, their next trial would begin soon after they left this site.

CHAPTER 5

Struggling to Reach Scroggie Creek

Evening was approaching and they had to cross a large creek with water flowing over the ice. The water was disappearing and then reappearing in a bizarre manner. Continuous flooding and freezing had made a plateau of ice, built up in irregular shapes.

Layer upon layer had widened the ice patch up and beyond the natural creek banks, so that the banks themselves were no longer visible. This phenomenon of nature is hard to explain. One has to see it to appreciate the difficult and precarious situation it presents for anyone that must cross it.

Don stood on higher dry spots in order to plan a route across. The men's biggest concern was that they might inadvertently break through the ice with either the John Deere or the trailer bearing all of their supplies. They chose their course with utmost caution. They managed to get approximately one-third of the distance across when all of a sudden – plunk! – the right wheel of the trailer dropped through the ice. The bed of the trailer on that side was actually flat on the ice. A closer look showed that the wheel of the trailer was in a water hole. The bulldozer would only spin in its tracks – they were undeniably seriously stuck.

Don unhooked the John Deere and began solemnly thinking about what approach might work best. If he took the machine to the back of the trailer, it might cause even more ice to break because of the extra weight of the John Deere. Then both the trailer and the John Deere would be stuck in the ice and submerged in water.

After measuring it, Forrest and Don found out that there was about five feet of water where the wheel had gone through. Next, with the axe and chisel they tested the ice around the trailer. Fortunately it was several feet thick, sufficient to support the bulldozer while it lifted the back corner of the trailer. They realized that the trailer wheel had found the only weak spot in the surrounding ice.

After lifting up the back of the trailer with the John Deere blade, they placed a piece of log under it. Then, with the aid of the winch line, they managed to get the trailer out of the hole. By this time they realized that they should never have had a two-wheel, rubber-tired trailer for this kind of trip.

It was now quite dark, so the men had to pick their way across the rest of the ice with only the aid of the machine's lights. After successfully accomplishing this, they wound their way through trees and found a suitable spot to camp for the night. Both realized that they were lucky to get out of that mishap.

Remarkably, although they were extremely tired and hungry, they were able to maintain a fairly cheerful attitude. In fact, at no time did either of the men even contemplate giving up, and all things considered, God only knew how long this trip was going to take them. In fact, on many occasions, either one of the two could be heard wondering aloud, "Will we ever get there?"

On this particular evening, one thing was in their favour. The weather had moderated somewhat. This, and the open water at the creek, made washing up easier and more pleasant than usual. In fact, they were able to treat themselves to the luxury of a hot-water hand and face wash. Of course, daily showers or baths had become a forgotten luxury. The best they could do was a partial stripdown, hitting only the spots that showed.

Their unshaven faces made them look and feel like a couple of 1898 prospectors, with the common route leading to a common goal – the gold-bearing creeks of the Yukon. Fortunately, Preparation H continued to help their cracked, sore lips. They had an abundant supply of clean clothes, but due to the extremely cold weather, they had changed their underclothes very few times. This night was no exception. The two exhausted men climbed into their sleeping bags wearing all their clothes, excluding only their snowmobile suits and boots.

Although they were unaware of it, the following day was one of four still to go. Progress was to continue at a slow rate. The nature of the country was changing, though. There was still about the same amount of snow but the ground was much more open now. It looked as if a fire had gone through the area in the not too distant past. It was in this region that they first spotted caribou tracks. Prior to this, they had come across coyote, rabbit, squirrel and the occasional fox tracks. Once they had even seen wolf tracks, and that very evening for hours Don and Forrest had heard the eerie howls of the wolves. Although they were in Peter Isaac's trapping territory, they had yet to see any signs of activity on his trapline.

It was shortly after spotting the caribou tracks that they received their first communication from the outside world since leaving Pelly ranch. A helicopter swooped low from the sky, right in front of them. The pilot came near enough to take a good look at them. When Don and Forrest waved, he knew that they were okay, and off he went. On this trip they had not thought to take a radio. In the future it would be a definite comfort to them.

The open area they were now in made it far easier to choose a route. They began climbing a fairly long, winding, steep hill which would eventually lead them into the Walhalla Valley. Their short-lived reprieve from complications was going to come to a halt, and their perseverance and intact tempers were going to be put to more tough tests. The temperature was beginning to drop rapidly, which meant that, as before, the machine could not be shut off at any time. They had consumed much more fuel than they had anticipated, so once again they resolved that they would have to travel day and night. Besides, they were far behind schedule and were now beginning to run low on food, so they could see no alternative.

They still had no idea how much longer it would take them to arrive at Scroggie, and knew that they could not go on indefinitely without sleep. They decided that, while one of them drove the machine, cleared the road ahead, and then returned to the trailer, the other would sleep in a sleeping bag under the tarp on top of the load. He would get woken up in time to help the other back up the John Deere, and guide him carefully to where the pin needed to be dropped into the trailer hitch. Once done, the driver could suspend his responsibilities and snatch his portion of sleep time.

Exchanging places in this way enabled them to go around the clock, though the night-time temperature was now -40°F. The quality eider-down sleeping bags they had bought and their snowmobile suits, which

30 *Rivers of Gold*

never left their bodies now, were invaluable. One of the hardest things they had to do was leave their sleeping bags when their turn came to drive. In fact, on one occasion, Don wondered if he would ever be able to get Forrest to leave his bag – he had one heck of a time trying to get him mobile.

All in all, they remained amazingly civil towards one another. Astounding determination was going to be required of them if they were to have any chance of completing this trip, and each seemed to understand and respect the inner struggles of the other. There were times, though, that it did seem hopeless. With all of Don's bush experience he had never contemplated anything like this. It had been two weeks since they had left Pelly Ranch, and a mere 35 miles had been covered.

They finally broke over the crest and began to descend into the Walhalla Valley. Walhalla Creek leads into, and then becomes, Scroggie Creek. Although a creek is often visualized as small, many of the creeks in this area were more like rivers. According to the map, when they reached the bottom of the valley their next landmark, Pyroxene Mountain, should be in view. There was a slight improvement in weather, and the next few days passed fairly uneventfully. They struggled and fought their way down to the bottom of the valley, and for the first time they were absolutely sure where they were. There, on their left, was the documented Pyroxene Mountain. With renewed confidence, Don and Forrest decided they could now revert back to being on the same day-and-night schedule.

As had become the norm on this trip, Murphy's Law would intervene again. Forrest was taking a turn on the John Deere while Don was making Sapporo soup. Don happened to look up and saw Forrest, looking despondent, coming towards him on foot.

"Now what in hell!" exclaimed Don.

"I've broken through ice in a swampy area," Forrest revealed, "and the bulldozer has its ass end buried and front end sticking up."

The two went back to survey the situation and decided they'd have to get the winch line out. Instead of winching straight back, they chose to winch sideways, as there was a suitable tree they could use as an anchor. It was a wise decision, because with winching, and the tracks turning, the bulldozer crawled out.

All was still not well. They soon discovered bolts missing from the rollers of the machine; others were loose. They did what they could, improvising and using the limited tools they had, but soon realized that a suitable repair job could never be accomplished. What could they do? They knew that if they continued driving there was a good chance they could cause further harm to the John Deere, possibly damaging it beyond repair.

With an estimated ten miles left to Scroggie, they had no choice but to leave both the John Deere and trailer where they were. They cleared a spot for the trailer and the John Deere, and then another one large enough for the helicopter that would have to return Don to this spot in the spring. He would have to bring the necessary tools, do a proper repair job, and complete the last of the trek to Scroggie Creek at that time.

Forrest and Don unloaded the snowmobiles and the little sled and began preparing for their trip back to Pelly Ranch. They packed the sled with their sleeping bags, extra gas for the snowmobiles and survival rations. At 3 p.m. they set off for the ranch. What a difference to be travelling at snowmobile speed! Don had never ridden a snowmobile before but was evidently a quick learner. Later he would discover a few sore muscles related to this new activity, but felt they were a cheap price to pay for the reward of speedy travel.

Their primary concern became the little sled attached to the back of Don's snowmobile. It continued to flip over at intervals along the way. Apart from this, the men made good time considering the glaciers and sections of open water they had to contend with.

They soon came to the creek where they had damaged the sidearm of the machine. Minutes later they broke out over the valley and saw the lights of Pelly Ranch below. What a welcoming sight! They arrived shortly before midnight and the Bradleys, who had seen the approaching snowmobile lights, came out to greet them. Don and Forrest had little trouble coming to a unanimous decision to accept the Bradleys' offer of hospitality. Don undid the sleeping bags, and to his consternation discovered that the gas container had developed a hole and had completely saturated one of the bags. How fortunate that they would not have to sleep outdoors that night!

It was wonderful to be in civilization again with good company,

The bulldozer goes through the ice on the trip to Scroggie.

Snowmobiling back to civilization

hot food and hot water. However, tiredness soon won over, and the superb conversation they were sharing came to an end. It was hard to believe that they were finally going to be able to fall asleep in the warmth of the indoors. Forrest used the intact sleeping bag and Don retired to the comfort of a bed. With temperatures at -20°F in the morning, it took some effort for the two men to push themselves away from the breakfast table in order to go outdoors to start up the snowmobiles.

The timing of their visit turned out to have an added benefit. They had met Shawn, a likable young fellow who was staying at Pelly Ranch at the time. After finding out that he had worked in trapping, farming and outfitting, and that he loved both the Yukon and the bush, the wheels began turning in Don's head. He asked Shawn if he would like to work for him at Scroggie Creek on Don's return to the Yukon. Shawn readily accepted. The people at Pelly Ranch had been obliging in so many ways. Don and Forrest warmly thanked the Bradleys for everything, left their generous hosts, and headed on towards Pelly Crossing.

About ten miles from Pelly Crossing they came upon a mill where logging activity was happening. Don and Forrest stopped to talk with one of the native Canadians they saw. He told them that part of the road to Pelly Crossing had very little snow on it, which would be hard on the snowmobiles. He kindly offered to put one of their machines and the sled on his truck. Unfortunately there was room for only one, so Don offered to take his chances with the road. Forrest put his snowmobile and the little sled on the man's truck, and drove on ahead with him to where he had left his own Peterbilt.

Taking great care, Don carried on, sometimes having to go into the ditch in order to find sufficient snow. About two miles from Pelly Crossing he came to a stretch of road with absolutely no snow on it. With no possibility of travelling where there was any, Don had to keep going right down the middle. At one point, he roared around a corner, rocks and sparks flying from metal ice picks on the treads contacting gravel, and came upon a woman walking a big dog. As he passed by her, he caught a glimpse of her startled face. He was sure she must have been thinking, "What kind of a madman is this? Who would race down a gravel road on a snowmobile?"

Don couldn't stop and explain, though, as only his momentum

was keeping him going. He was shortly back on ice and crossing Pelly River to rendezvous with Forrest and his new friend.

By this time Forrest was trying unsuccessfully to start his Peterbilt tractor, and was running down his battery in the process. His friend once again came to his rescue with jumper cables and a few shots of ether. With the truck fired up, the snowmobiles were quickly loaded and tied down, and Don and Forrest were on the road again.

When they arrived in Whitehorse they checked into the Airport Chalet. On the top of both of their lists was a long hot bath with lots and lots of soap. Don went first, and after cleaning up the tub, it was Forrest's turn for a much needed scrubdown. Once both were clean and refreshed they sat down and relaxed. Forrest's relaxation lasted only a few moments, as a short while later Don re-entered the bathroom and immediately hollered, "Forrest, get the hell in here and clean this tub! The way you've left it, it looks like you changed the Peterbilt oil in it." So clean it Forrest did.

The next thing on their wish list was food. They went to the hotel's restaurant where each ordered the biggest steak on the menu, along with all the trimmings. Both of them devoured their huge platters with gusto and each claimed it to be the very best steak he had ever eaten. It was certainly a wonderful and welcome change from one-pot dinners and the near-starvation they'd become accustomed to in the bush. In fact, both Don and Forrest had lost considerable weight since they left home.

Dinner done, they went back to their room and called home to let us know they were back in civilization and comfortable for the first time in a month. Then it was lights out and a sound sleep for both.

They rose early, anxious to get on their way and to put an end to this trying trip. They travelled down the Alaska Highway to the Cassiar Highway junction, then headed south, following the same route they had taken up to the Yukon. They encountered the usual winter road conditions, but otherwise were happy to report an uneventful trip. Once home safe, and very relieved to be there, they were able to acknowledge that they had accomplished what, at many times, seemed impossible.

CHAPTER 6

Building the Camp at Scroggie

At the beginning of April 1979, Don had been home from his trip for only a few days when already he began thinking of the next one. After all, it was only a little over a month before he would be heading out again. This time our son, Brian, planned on going with him to our mining claims. I would join Don there a month after, and Brian would came back to Langley to take over managing Lee's Jade and Opals.

We were still operating on a limited budget and couldn't afford to make any big mistakes, so we put a great deal of consideration into the planning of this trip. We had to purchase three tents. One would be used as a cookhouse, another as sleeping quarters and the third as storage for the mining supplies. It was also necessary to buy three large metal trunks to store our food stocks. This would keep them dry and free from mice and other rodents. After what had happened to Don and Forrest on their last trip, we knew we couldn't skimp on sleeping bags either. This time, along with one good sleeping bag, we were each going to have a couple of spares.

To save on costs, we gathered many of the household items, towels and sheets we would need from family and friends. We told them that if they were going to throw anything out, to throw it our way first. I made sure that all of the cooking and daily-living requirements would be met, while Don looked after everything that would be required for prospecting and mining. By the beginning of May, as we had planned, everything was ready for the trip north.

Don and Brian drove the three-quarter-ton pickup truck loaded with supplies to Dawson City. From there they had the supplies flown to the small Scroggie airstrip in a Twin Otter aircraft. Brian was left to guard the goods at the airstrip, while Don went back to Dawson to meet Shawn. From there, Don and Shawn took a helicopter out to the place where Don and Forrest had been forced to leave the John Deere bulldozer and trailer in March.

While Don and Shawn properly repaired the machine, the helicopter pilot flew several loads of gear from the abandoned rubber-tired trailer to the Scroggie airstrip. Shawn flew out with it on its last trip to Scroggie Creek, where he would await Don's arrival. On his own, Don was going to drive the John Deere and trailer to the airstrip, where Brian was waiting.

Meanwhile Brian had gotten the flu. Don said poor Brian had made a hole among the supplies and crawled in to lie down and await Don's return. Little did Brian know he would be waiting a long time. Don was dogged with his usual ill luck. He had managed to do two or three miles, when to his dismay, the trailer tipped over, load and all. It was a mess. He had only one option. He unhitched the trailer, picked up his .44 Magnum revolver, and began walking to the airstrip.

It was late afternoon as Don slogged through the muck, mud and water. He was thankful he had the gun when he saw a "big timer" wolf cross the trail directly in front of him. Don didn't have to use his gun, because all the wolf did was stand at the edge of the bush and observe him.

A few miles further on he came to Walhalla Creek. Not knowing how deep it would be, he chose the spot he felt would be the most shallow, stripped off his clothes, put them and his gun over his head, and crossed the icy water – a distance of 40 to 50 feet – to the bank on the other side. It was waist deep at points. With chattering teeth and shaking hands, Don put his clothing back on his numbed body. It was pitch black out by now. He carried on in the darkness, and finally arrived at the Scroggie airstrip around midnight.

With Brian still very ill, and both extremely tired and hungry, they climbed into their sleeping bags to get some rest. The next morning they used their radio to enlist help. Don had concluded that lessening the weight was the only way he could get the John Deere and trailer through the terrain to the airport. It was necessary for them to bring in the helicopter yet another time, in order to get the goods from the upset trailer over. This completed, Don went back once again and with the aid of the winch line on the John Deere managed to get the trailer upright. Thus the John Deere caterpillar, the trailer and Don all finally made it to the Scroggie airstrip together.

Their next task was to take, load by load, the assorted goods from the little airstrip to the Scroggie campsite. The sight of the mixed mess of goods piled up at the runway was close to impossible to describe. There was prospecting equipment and tents and items for housing and food provisions. It looked like it would take forever to transport. At the campsite there were many things to be taken care of, too, including setting up tents and building an outhouse. However, Don, Brian and Shawn tackled it all with enthusiasm, one day at a time. They knew that each job accomplished was getting them nearer and nearer to what they had come here to do – mine for gold.

During this time they had the opportunity to enjoy the benefits that came with this natural outdoor environment that all three of them thrived on. The animals became their neighbours. A flicker that had made its nest in a poplar tree became a daily point of interest. They hadn't realized when they had tied the tent ridgepole to the tree that they would be sharing the tree with the flicker and her young. They were able to share in the joy of watching the little ones reach maturity and leave the nest. Other animal neighbours included a black bear – on several occasions seen very close to the camp – and a moose that they nicknamed "Moses."

When Don and Brian and Shawn had been at Scroggie for almost a month, I sent word to Don that my cousin and spouse were going to be arriving from England to visit for a few weeks. Don decided he would fly out with Brian, spend a few days with our visitors and then fly to the Cry Lake Jade Mine, near Dease Lake in northwestern B.C. He had the job of marketing the jade for its owner, Mohawk Oil. After that the two of us would go back to Scroggie Creek together. Don left Shawn in charge of the camp and he and Brian came home.

It was July 10th, almost midway through the Yukon mining season, when Don and I left together on our flight back. We had to stop and spend a few hours in Whitehorse waiting for the plane that would take us on to Dawson. I was dressed in a smart pantsuit and shoes with two-inch heels. Don looked down at my feet and asked, "What shoes did you bring to walk from the airstrip to camp?"

Preparing the way into Scroggie Creek.

Brian and Shawn testing gravel at Scroggie Creek.

"Just what I've got on," I replied.

"Well, you sure aren't walking that ground in those shoes," he said. "Let's get a taxi right now and get into Whitehorse to buy you something sensible." That's just what we did. Low-heeled, closed-toe, good utilitarian walking shoes were soon on my feet. We spent a few more minutes browsing in a large bookstore, and after I purchased a few pocket books, we headed back to the airport to catch the DC-3 plane for Dawson.

It was a twenty-passenger plane but there were only about ten people and a few cargo boxes on board. The plane landed briefly in Mayo, but so many changes had taken place since 1951 that neither of us could pick out anything familiar. Both Whitehorse and Dawson temperatures had soared, and most of the conversation on the plane seemed to revolve around complaints of the heat. Don and I hoped the good weather would continue. We knew we would need it when we arrived at the camp and began working outdoors all day. We were glad to see the sun still shining as we stepped out of the plane at Dawson at 10 p.m.

Don had made reservations for us at Ursula Oltman's Dawson cabins. Ursula was young, energetic and very obliging. Since she was also the expediter, she relayed to us the radio conversations she'd had with Shawn. She told us that he would be at the Scroggie airstrip to meet Don and me when we landed. We flew out the following morning in a 206 Cessna. I sat up front because Don said that way I'd get a better view of how they had set up the camp. After seeing miles of forest, creeks and hills, the colourful tarps, tents and cabins at the camp were a welcoming sight.

As promised, Shawn was at the airstrip. The first thing he said was, "It's rained a lot the fourteen days you've been gone, Don."

Our pilot took a look around and then helped us unload the supplies. Then he said he had to be off, and left us with what seemed to be an apologetic look for abandoning us in the wilderness. I was unaffected at this point. It was a sunny day with the bluest of blue skies. A profusion of wild flowers bloomed – wild roses in shades of pink, lupines, yellow daisies, bluebells, mauve cosmos types, white flowers that looked like baby's breath and of course fireweed, the floral emblem of the Yukon. It seemed to me that the flowers up here had deeper hues. They were beautiful. I felt happy to be here, surrounded by this ravishing wilderness.

Don, Shawn and I decided to walk to camp. Don could return later with the bulldozer and trailer to load up the supplies we had brought, along with the metal roofing and plywood that needed to be brought to the camp. I couldn't get over the view. I kept glancing up at the hills. Some were bare rock schist and others were covered in trees. There were so many bees and wasps. They seemed to be in every tree, on every foot of ground and all around us in the air, yet somehow they managed to keep out of our way. It made me think of our son, Brian.

"I'm sure glad Brian isn't here right now," I said. "He's very allergic to bee stings. I'm allergic to a lesser degree, but I'll still have to be on constant guard." With the profusion of flowers, no pollution in the air and the great number of bees around, I wondered why there were no apiaries in the Yukon. I learned later it was because the winters were too severe for honeybees.

Upon reaching the Scroggie campsite, Shawn and Don gave me a tour. I was impressed with all that had been accomplished. It was getting late in the day and we were all exhausted. I decided that while Don went back to collect the supplies, I'd make up a quick spaghetti dinner so that we could all retire early. We would need to keep up our energy for working in the days ahead.

CHAPTER 7

Admiring Our First Nuggets

Each day at Scroggie brought with it more and more experience. Shawn, Don and I were slowly beginning to feel like true Yukon placer miners. We were acquiring a vocabulary connected to the North and gold mining such as stripping, sluicing, tunnelling, hydraulicing, panning, claims, chechako, Chilkoot, Bonanza and Discovery. These words took on new meaning for us. They now conjured up a picture for us of what Dawson must have been like in its heyday.

Our increasing knowledge, together with the development of certain routines, gradually enabled us to get more done in a shorter time period. In fact, we had adopted a fairly stable daily routine that was working well for all of us. It went something like this.

Without fail, rising time seven days a week was 6 a.m. Immediately each of us washed our faces and hands with the cold-water basin that had been set on a stump. One thing I insisted on was that each person have their own hand soap and keep it in their own empty plastic margarine containers. I said, "If you like to use dirty soap you can, but I'm not." Consequently, however you left your bar of soap – dirty or rinsed off – was how you found it the next time.

Next I made breakfast, always as healthy and interesting as possible, while Don and Shawn started the bulldozer and did chores such as filling the diesel-fuel tank on the pump or making a trip for drinking water. The men went to work immediately after breakfast while I did the dishes, cleaned and prepared foods for meals later in the day. A coffee break was taken around 10 a.m. and again at 3 p.m. Lunch was always the previous night's leftovers. If the day was cool the leftovers usually went into a soup. On a hot day they became part of a salad.

Supper was always between 6 and 6:30 p.m. Many suppers were slow-simmered stews that I could start when I made the 3 p.m. coffee.

Whether the men worked at digging and sluicing after supper depended on the weather and at what stage they had left their work. If they didn't go back to mining, they attacked the never-ending list of spare-time jobs. Nine-thirty to 10 o'clock was shower time. This was followed by our ritual of having coffee or hot chocolate before bed. Shawn and I were both coffee lovers, but Don liked hot chocolate.

Of course there were exceptions to our routine. There were some things we had no control over. For instance, we never knew when the helicopter would bring in our supplies. Sometimes we had just gotten to sleep when we heard the woomph-woomph of the helicopter motor and blades. We'd make a frantic dash to get dressed and put a pot of coffee on so that we were ready to greet the pilot. Breaks like these were actually welcome. In these brief visits, we caught up on news of Dawson and the rest of the Yukon.

Unlike the sparse Yukon news, we could often get the world news. This we would hear, usually late in the evening, on Don's short-wave radio. Our expediter, Ursula, also periodically checked in on us to see how things were. We had arranged with her to listen for messages between 7 and 8 o'clock, morning and evening. In these calls relevant news was relayed both ways. It was always good to hear her voice and it made us think, "Gee, we're not that far from civilization after all." A warm feeling always came over me with this realization.

With the many things that could go wrong, a radio was more than a comfort for today's prospectors. It was a real necessity. Making arrangements for fuel and groceries to be brought in to us was one of its many uses.

The trip from Dawson City to our camp and back with a Jet Ranger helicopter cost approximately $600 each time. This helicopter was able to bring only two 45-gallon drums of fuel at a time, plus groceries. Our propane also had to be flown in, so careful thought was made every time the helicopter was ordered. Of course, there were always emergency helicopter trips necessary because of equipment breakdowns.

This was a "Mom and Pop" operation, not an international mining venture, so cost was a major consideration in everything. Once in a while, thoughts of money, work and everything else that could prey on one's mind were suspended. These were the times when the magnificence of the North and its unique allure could take one's breath away. There were many phenomena, strange and beautiful, in this land: the huge, round, fiery ball of the midnight sun, the ceaseless daylight of the summer months and the aurora borealis (the northern lights).

Frequent rain showers, while the sun still shone, made it a summer of rainbows. Beautiful wide bands of colour spanned the sky and seemed to end in the valley. It was almost as if the end of the rainbow really did point to the fabled pot of gold. In one day it was not uncommon to have a mix of weather: sun, clouds, thunder, rain and then more sunshine.

One night at approximately midnight, while it was still daylight, I stepped outside the tent to see a sky that was carrying the most beautiful clouds in one direction, and large black ominous clouds in the other. What a contrast! I called, "Don, come and see this beautiful sky," but he declined and snuggled further into the warm bed, professing that he was too tired.

Our Scroggie site was really starting to shape up. Although we certainly didn't have the luxuries we were used to at home in Langley, the camp was becoming more and more livable. In the sleeping tent that Don and I occupied, a pole framework supported our mattress. There was a clothes rack, also made of poles. Shelves sported plastic curtains. The rainy weather tended to make the tent quite damp. This was offset by using a small propane heater sparingly. Shawn had more luxury than us – he actually had an airtight heater in his cabin.

The cookhouse tent had a freestanding counter covered in linoleum which also served as a table. Under the counter sat the three large metal trunks, holding all the food that we feared the mice might attack. Canned goods, cleaning fluids, cooking utensils and dishes were stored on freestanding shelves covered with colourful plastic curtains that hid the crudeness of the shelving.

All in all, it looked quite bright and cheerful. Our collection of supplies and utensils included a little oven that fit on the top of the three-burner propane stove. One morning I decided to try to make biscuits. Don and Shawn said they were yummy. Having them turn out so well took away any excuse I had not to try buns and pies. Making these was now added to my list of spare-time jobs. How that list continued to grow!

One thing most people enjoy is taking a shower – even more so after working hard during the day. But how do you have a shower with no plumbing, especially if you want piped hot water? Don solved this problem by making what we called our "Yukon shower."

He located four trees that made a six- to eight-foot square. Next he took the boughs off eight feet high, stretched a tarp around the outside of the four trunks, leaving an opening for an entrance. A few poles made a partial roof, which became a platform for a five-gallon pail which held the shower water. This pail was painted black inside and out. The dark colour attracted and held the radiant energy of the sunlight. A hole was cut in the bottom and a pipe fitting put in with a valve and shower head.

The floor was made of small poles laid horizontally; spaces between them allowed the water to go through and enter a small ditch which led the used water away. We climbed a ladder mounted on the outside to put hot water in the bucket. Then we could go inside to undress. On one trunk there were spikes to hang the towel and our clothes on. Another tree held the soap container – usually a margarine dish with a couple of holes punched in the bottom. Once the shower valve was opened, we got whatever temperature of water was in the five-gallon pail. There was nothing to adjust – whatever we put in and the sun heated, came out. This shower was luxury indeed.

The only drawback to our Yukon shower was that most of the roof was open to the skies, so, while we had privacy at ground level, we didn't from above. I had to hastily finish my shower if I heard the droning of a helicopter motor becoming loud enough to suggest it was close.

Although our site was improving, there were still many things that reminded us of how grateful we should be for the conveniences we had at home. Housekeeping was one of these for me. It was definitely not easy here. For one thing, we had to pack water from Scroggie Creek about 350 feet away, and it was all uphill when we had full buckets. We used this for cooking and drinking. Our wash water and shower water was taken from a scooped out pond which filled with water naturally.

Laundry was another extremely difficult chore. I did the laundry with an old scrub board and a series of washtubs. It was a time-consuming job that was required several times a week. Have you ever seen pictures of the pioneer women toiling over a ridged-glass scrub board, set in a galvanized tub? This was exactly how I had to do the laundry. I filled the first tub with hot soapy water. Taking a few clothes at a time, I put them into the water. Then I rubbed them over the ridges of the scrub board until they were clean. Next, I put them into one of the tubs of rinse water.

Extracting the surplus water from some of the items was too difficult for me to do by myself. For these, I'd call one of the men to aid me. We'd each take one end of the article and twist in opposite directions. Once we got most of the excess water out, I'd hang the article on a rope that was strung between two trees. It was often windy, so the clothes dried fluffy and sweet-smelling from the fresh outdoor air.

When you wash clothes by hand, it's very difficult to get the dirt out. For this reason, I preferred to do it more often rather than deal with a few really filthy clothes. Unlike the pioneers, one thing I had to be thankful for was having store-bought soap. Just imagine if I'd had to make my own soap too!

The same washtub that I used for washing clothes had served as our bathtub previous to the building of the Yukon shower. Every evening I took orders for each bath, so that I could get a head start heating up the water on the three-burner propane stove. One thing I always insisted on was everyone regularly bathing and changing their clothes.

On top of the many routine chores we all had, there were many other spare jobs that needed completing. The list for these jobs seemed to get longer and longer. I didn't know how we would ever get it all done. One job that we felt was a priority was fixing up the second cabin sufficiently to house extra supplies. We needed somewhere to store them over the winter.

This year our main objectives had been to set the camp up, do the required assessment work for the current year, and determine where we should concentrate working the next year. Since prospecting and testing is required to locate the best place to commence serious mining, this was what a majority of our time was spent doing.

Testing, in our small mining operation, meant using small-scale equipment, usually hand-operated. One took a few shovelfuls of the gravel, washed it by putting it in a gold pan or through a small sluice-box. This sluice-box was small enough to be carried on one's back. Washing the gravel until all pieces larger than pea-size were removed left only very fine gravel, black sand and gold as residue. This residue we put through the gold spinner, which separated the gold from the other material. Hence we were able to collect it and evaluate the amount of gold retrieved in relation to the quantity of gravel we used in the test.

The next step was to move to another location and go through the same procedure. One can systematically work from one end of the property to the other and reap whatever gold comes, but testing helps to indicate where it will be most profitable to begin the actual mining and get monetary returns more quickly.

We were getting a lot of rain and we had one heavy thunder-and-lightning storm. This was making it more difficult for Don, who was working with the bulldozer. He had been pushing overburden to one side, and then, when the gold-bearing gravel was reached, it was put through the sluice-box. There were lots of yellow rocks in this place, small ones that made us think of nuggets and got our hearts to thumping. They were only a tease, though, for they were nothing but river gravel. Us "chechakos" – the 1898 Gold Rush term given to new-comers to the Yukon – still had a lot left to learn. It certainly was a mean country for beginners.

While Don worked the bulldozer, Shawn did handyman work. I didn't like being that far in the bush very much – I was terrified a bear might visit. Whenever the two of them were going to be working more than 100 yards from camp, I went with them. If they were in the near vicinity of the camp, I was able to get cleaning, cooking and laundry done. If not, I waited until evening when the men were back to do these chores.

Testing various areas of ground and putting the concentrate through the gold spinner was producing some gold nuggets. In a water hole, Don put in the shovel and got it as full of gravel as possible. He put this through the sluice and then the spinner and we were amazed at the size of two of the nuggets. Don quickly got the John Deere in motion and dug up more dirt in preparation for the following day's work. However, after putting it through the sluice and spinner, there was very little additional gold. We had to conclude that the gold probably came from the previous day, and the nuggets had got caught in the spinner.

We continued doing our prospecting and testing, still hunting for the best place to initiate diligent mining. We had two, two-inch pumps, with plenty of two-inch discharge hose. This enabled us to bring the water a considerable distance to wherever we had set up the testing sluice-box. We were prospecting on a bench approximately 100-125 feet above the present creek. We presumed that the original creek was this bench, and here was deposited all the gold-bearing gravel. It was impossible to find the exact channel of the old creek, because Mother Nature was constantly changing the terrain.

We found it fascinating that the early 20th-century prospectors and miners had mined with only hand tools. In one place, there was evidence of horses pulling slips. (A slip is a two-handed scoop.) You could load or unload by movement of the handles up or down.

It was obvious that there had been careful thought and work put into the water system for their sluicing. We saw open ditches which would lead the water from a higher elevation to the place that they were sluicing. The ditches at Scroggie are up to a mile long. A wooden trough or flume replaced the ditch in the rocky sections, where they could not dig a ditch to transport the water to the gravel they were washing.

At another site we found remnants of towers – one near a creek and the other uphill, equipped with cable and buckets in between. We assumed that they'd sent the gravel down to the creek for washing. All gold-bearing gravel requires washing in order for the gold to settle to the bottom and be retrieved. With this system it was also possible that they could send something uphill, provided the downhill weight was greater. Sluicing as described above can only be done from late spring to fall, as it requires weather warm enough so that the water will flow.

The tools that we found had been handmade by a blacksmith. The variety of things that had been made on site surprised us: spikes, tongs, pins, hinges, shovels, picks, axes and anything else they required at any given moment.

For the people who stayed through the winter and continued to work, their only option was to light fires to thaw a few inches of ground at a time, remove the muck, and put it in a waste pile. When they hit the gold-bearing gravel and got down to bedrock, the material was stockpiled for sluicing in the spring. Doing this in several locations put them ahead for the next spring. They chose several areas from which they would pan out a few panfuls; this helped them determine where the richest ground was to do the sluicing in the spring. Working through the winter also prevented "cabin fever."

We continued to have a lot of rainy days, making working conditions miserable, but we were encouraged by finding some coarse gold nuggets in our testing. Most of the time we were working up the hill about 300 yards from camp. Don was busy doing a section of stripping, taking the overburden off. At the first chance we got, we put some through the small sluice-box and panned out the concentrates to see how much gold was there. It was fascinating to see the little nuggets and flecks in the bottom of the pan.

After the first find of gold, we could understand the saying, "bitten by gold fever." It brought to mind Robert Service's poem, "The Spell of the Yukon," with the lines, "Yet it isn't gold that I'm wanting so much as just finding the gold." How true this was.

We decided to do a little more testing before moving to another spot. Don was shovelling, Shawn was raking the gravel through the small sluice-box, and I was at the end of the chute keeping the gravel away after it was washed. I jokingly told them, "I'll stay here so I can gather the big nuggets the sluice didn't catch." Needless to say, I did not have to stoop for a single nugget.

Working small sections at a time helped us to pinpoint the most productive areas. Don would make a small catch basin for the surplus water. Next, the small sluice-box would be set up and the gravel shovelled into it. It was washed, and then the concentrate was put through the gold spinner. We all had our eyes glued on the final panning. We were almost spellbound when we beheld the little nuggets. After each area that we tested, we tabulated the results in our workbook before moving on to the next test area.

Days passed quickly and it was time we gave some thought to going over to Barker Creek to do the assessment work on that lease. Brian had inquired of the Yukon Government if we could pay cash in lieu of doing the assessment work, as we'd had such rainy weather and the ground would be difficult to travel on. The answer was a definite no – we had to physically do the work. In B.C. a person had the option to pay the value of the assessment work, instead of physically doing work of the assessment value. The law in the Yukon was different.

CHAPTER 8

Breaking Ground at Barker Creek

In preparing for the trip to Barker Creek, we had to think carefully about all the articles and supplies we would need, as we would be isolated for most of the week. We would be using the bulldozer as our mode of transportation for the distance of 25 miles. It would be necessary to cross Scroggie Creek twice. One or two other creeks would also be crossed.

Don took the cat down to Scroggie Creek to select a good place to cross the next morning. He went through the creek, and bladed out the further bank so it would be less steep. With that prepared, he returned to the camp to load the John Deere. Don drilled holes in the roof and bolted his tool box to it. On a platform over the winch was a barrel of fuel, cans and supplies, and sleeping bags. Packboards and tarps were strapped onto the sides of the cab, along with axes, shovels and a chainsaw. Placed on the hydraulic tank was a cooler chest full of groceries, and another one full of kitchen supplies.

The radio, rifles, camera and everything else were stuffed wherever possible. Last, but not least, there had to be room for the passengers – Shawn and myself.

Now that we were packed for Barker Creek, we had to consider how we should leave Scroggie. We had already put things safely away, in case of mice, gophers, bears, etc. invading the camp while we were away. Our main concern was the cookhouse. We now took all of our canned goods and put them into Shawn's log cabin. Everything possible was cleared off the shelves and put in our metal trunks. Everything looked fine. Although we hadn't been bothered yet by our neighbour, the black bear (or any of his relatives), and didn't really expect to be, we still felt the need to keep a clean camp. After all, cooking and food odours do travel.

For the first ten miles Shawn was going to ride the motorcycle.

Don staking claims.

Don on bulldozer loaded for the trip to Barker Creek.

We decided we would leave it in the bush before we made the second crossing of Scroggie. Then, if there were any problems, there would be some kind of backup transportation. What a sight our bulldozer "bus" made! I had prepared a lot of sandwiches so we could eat while on the move. We all thought we had planned the trip out perfectly. We felt that the sunshine brightening the day was a good omen.

We followed the stagecoach trail. There were a lot of rubble-covered sections where Don had to use the blade to clear the way. I took snapshots of the beautiful scenery from my perch on the cat. Rock slides were fairly deep in some places and there were deep holes too. In places where the roadside had crumbled away, it took skilful blading, filling and maneuvering on Don's part to keep going.

When we reached the ten-mile spot, Shawn hid the Suzuki motorbike in the trees where we would pick it up on our way back. Before crossing the creek, Don decided to make a 50-foot-square clearing for an emergency helicopter pad. This is where we left the stagecoach trail. Scroggie was in several places wider and deeper than many rivers, and also very fast-flowing, so Don carefully chose his crossing spot. The water came about two-thirds of the way up the machine's tracks, but all seemed to be going relatively well. We figured we'd be at Barker Creek by late afternoon.

We planned to do the work as quickly as possible, and then return on the John Deere back to Scroggie to resume our work there. These plans sure changed! After crossing Scroggie, Don headed for a poplar ridge, climbed to the top, and parked the bulldozer. Shawn and I walked for a while, allowing Don the time to plan his route and get his bearings. Don was like a homing pigeon when it came to direction, but seeing his concern, this was one time I began thinking we were lost for sure. We'd altered our course many times trying to avoid wet, boggy areas, and the continuous dodging in and out of trees made everything look alike.

When Don climbed a tree to get a better view of where we were, Shawn said, "Well, what do you see, Boss?"

"I see water, and for sure it's the Stewart River," replied Don. After several hours, the appreciation of the sunny bright day and the scenery and the trip had waned. By this time, we were all just wishing for the journey's completion. Seeing the Stewart River meant we were still on course.

We went back for the bulldozer, climbed aboard and on we went. Soon we came to an old wreck of a roadhouse, bearing a sign that read, "Barker Placer Mining Under Protection of Government of Yukon Territory." Robin Burian had claims next to ours, and it was from this point on the Stewart that he pulled his stoneboat of supplies to his cabin.

What muskeg this ground was! Many times we sank. Every place that the moss covering the permafrost was broken, the ground had begun to thaw and became a wet mess. Don worried that going over all the rocks and bumping along the stagecoach trail would wear the cat out. I figured the cat was the least of our worries. I was more afraid we were going to sink out of sight.

Don was beginning to think we'd better leave the cat, and walk out after doing our work. The only other alternative was to radio for a helicopter to come in for us. We could be heard at Robin's cabin and soon four people appeared. One was Robin. The others were Peggy, who now works with tourism in Dawson City, her husband and her sister. Can you imagine what they were thinking when out of the blue three people appeared, riding a bulldozer decked out like a gypsy caravan?

They invited our woebegone trio in for coffee, and with their permission we camped outdoors under a tree for the night. It was difficult to sleep as we were overtired, hungry and worried about what the route would be like the next day. We had food with us but were too tense to eat. Mosquitoes and bees were humming and flying around all night.

The following morning we made our breakfast over a small campfire. Robin came over to us and asked if we would like to see his workings. We readily accepted. We were amazed at the extent of his diggings. They were up to 20 feet deep. He had a D4 cat which we were soon to be very thankful for. Robin told us that he had made a trail to the end of his claims, that were bordering ours at Barker. When we left, this was what we began travelling on.

The trail, however, was bad in many places and we had to twist and turn snakelike to continue. We quickly learned just how bad travelling here could be. The bulldozer was sinking part way up its tracks in the mud and water-filled holes of the muskeg. Don had a difficult time operating the machine. I was sure it was only his expertise that kept us going. Slowly, we had made about three-quarters of a mile from Robin's cabin. Suddenly, there was a slope in the trail towards

Tent camp at Scroggie Creek.

Remains of old Barker Roadhouse.

Rivers of Gold

the creek immediately below. Don cleared the road somewhat, to lessen the slope, but the mud was like slippery ice. The bulldozer sallied sideways, almost tipping into the creek.

You may not believe this – a small willow tree held that bulldozer. It was leaning on a dangerous angle, but the tree prevented it, together with all our gear, from toppling into the creek. Don tied the winch line to the biggest tree he could find, but the weight of the bulldozer and load only uprooted the anchor tree and left the machine on an even more dangerous angle. What to do now?

Don is usually very independent and rarely asks for help, but this time I insisted that he seek aid. He tried to object, saying he could probably get us out of the predicament by putting the winch line across the creek and "sucking" us across. Then he could get level again and we'd be on our way.

This time I put my foot down. Emphatically, I said, "For once, swallow your pride and go and ask Robin for help! It's the only area that there is another cat that can help us, and it's foolish to risk losing our bulldozer and load. Do you realize what it will mean if that happens? Think of it. We won't be able to do our assessment work, let alone any mining. And we'll still require a lot of aid to get us out. If Robin comes now it's almost 100 percent sure we'll be out of this predicament."

After some thought, Don agreed to go and ask for Robin's help. Robin readily agreed, and in no time at all was there with his D4 cat. He crossed the creek and went past us on the opposite shoreline, crawled up the bank on our side, then positioned himself ahead on slightly higher ground. He attached the winch line from his cat to the John Deere, and with his winch in gear, and our tracks turning, we crawled out.

What a relief! I had been extremely nervous the whole time. I knew now what it meant to have your heart in your mouth from fear. Why, I believe that I chewed mine! We were deeply indebted to Robin. Fortunately, at a later date, we were able to return the favour.

This incident had set us behind by about two hours. We would continue travelling over Robin's trail on his placer claims on a route that required frequent crossing of Barker Creek. Each crossing had been carefully chosen for shallowness and a good gravel bottom. After we

Log cabin at Scroggie Creek.

The John Deere nearly upsets on the way to Barker Creek.

left Robin's claims, however, we would be breaking our own trail. We knew we'd have to cross Dixie Creek, which might present a problem.

Now, on our way again, the many ups and downs in the terrain had everyone tense. At times we made steep climbs, and it seemed as if we would turn over backwards. Other times we were going sideways on a steep angle. It made me very nervous. Deep water holes covered with soft mud and moss, which we sunk into, pushed panic buttons in me. Sometimes Don had to fill holes in with logs before we could continue. The bulldozer was constantly pushing over trees to make a road.

Don was hardly eating anything. I knew he was worried. Shawn was keeping very quiet and I was keeping all my fingers, and even my toes, crossed in hopes that we would safely meet our destination. We were so alone out here and, at this point, we were beyond where any machine had ever been. Were we not true pioneers?

Don was extremely careful when choosing which way to take. We often stopped the bulldozer, walked ahead to select safe – if there was such a thing – ground, checked everything, returned to the bulldozer and then proceeded. As we crossed another awful piece of muskeg ground, all I could think of was how this was anything but a pleasant trip. Many times we began to sink, and each time it seemed that this was the time we would get stuck for good. Then, like a miracle at the last moment, the tracks of the bulldozer would inch forward and we were on the go again.

We approached Dixie Creek. It was narrow, with straight banks about eight feet deep. There was no chance of cutting the banks down with the bulldozer blade. Don decided that he would cut a sufficient amount of trees, then place them in the creek horizontally until he had filled the creek enough to crawl across with the bulldozer. The trees, which were plentiful in this area, would not harm the creek. Water would run between and over the branches and trunks.

Don was pushing the trees when he noticed a helicopter overhead. It was the forestry. It circled, came back, and looked as if it was going to try to land. Don and Shawn quickly began cutting trees to clear a landing space. Off it went, circled again, followed their track, and then came back to them. It hovered and one of the passengers motioned to us, asking if we needed help. Don signalled that everything was okay, and off it went. We have often wondered what those in the chopper thought when they saw three people in a John Deere caravan, completely isolated, out on the muskeg in the heart of the Yukon wilderness.

It was now time to cross the creek. This was done without mishap. Next we had to decide whether to follow the valley bottom up to Iron Creek, or turn right, go up a steep hill, and get onto the bench which ran parallel to the river bottom. We chose the latter. We figured that it would be the shortest route to our destination, and it was already late afternoon. Now we were travelling along the bench. Don figured we were getting very close to our journey's end.

You must remember we had never seen this area except from the air. It was above our centre line, and nowhere near where we had walked while doing our staking the previous year. Don decided to stop the machine. At this point we found our gas can missing. We had to have it so that we could use the chain saw. Shawn offered to walk back and look for it, while Don walked ahead and checked the route. Luckily, Shawn found it a very short walk back.

We hoped Don was playing the role of Moses leading his people out of the wilderness, so Shawn and I followed in his footsteps. To our elation, Don pushed through the small but thick trees, and after going about a 100 feet saw a clearing and the old rock diggings on our lease.

Don levelled the rocks in an area big enough to set up a ridgepole covered with a tarp. This would be our camp. We looked across the valley to a pleasant view. A ridge on a hill showed a scattering of birch and poplar trees.

It was now 11 p.m. and we hadn't eaten since breakfast, but none of us was terribly hungry. The only thing we were feeling was relieved that we'd survived. Despite this, we made a campfire, had tea and put something into our stomachs. Then we collapsed into our sleeping bags. Despite the hard ground we had to sleep on, we all fell into a deep, desperately longed for, sleep.

The next morning we awoke to a cloudy sky, which soon converted into heavy torrential rain. This night we slept under another tarp, held up with a ridgepole, to help keep us dry. It wasn't enough to do the job. The ground itself had become saturated, and part way

Don and Gwen on the walk from Barker to Scroggie.

Cooking at Barker Creek camp.

through the night we awoke to find little rivulets beside our sleeping bags. We had to get up and build a trench around the exterior of the tarp. Wet and cold, we climbed back into our bags to await the morning.

Nothing was working well. The wood was green and wet, making it exceedingly difficult to start and keep a campfire going. We couldn't keep the fire burning sufficiently to heat our water and food. Thus the hotcakes I tried to make got voted the worst we'd ever eaten. The mosquitoes were very bad, so we had to keep a mosquito coil lit at all times. Effective as this was, we all detested the smell of it. We had no choice but to put up with one or the other. We hadn't had a decent wash since we'd left Scroggie, and we'd never been so dirty in our lives. In spite of it all we did our best to remain good-natured towards one another.

On just one occasion did Shawn lose his cool, but I could hardly blame him. He had hauled up the water and painstakingly got a nice fire going. In fact, on this occasion, it was burning so well that I thought I'd get a head start on heating up the water. I placed a pot of water on a rock near the fire, figuring the heat of the fire would give us a reserve of warm water when it was required.

I'm not sure how it happened, but the next thing I knew the pot had slipped from the rock and tipped over, putting out the hard fought for fire. All we ended up with was lots of smoke. Poor Shawn kicked that pot as far as he could, and let out a long string of cuss words. The rest of the day he remained silent. I apologized profusely, and spent the next hours kindling a fire and keeping it going.

The area that Don was working, doing the clearing and stripping, was growing and looking very impressive. Don was exceptionally pleased to see that the overburden was only two feet deep in some places. This would tremendously cut down on the hours of work required before being able to put the gravel through the sluice-box next spring. We found out later that there was not more than approximately six feet of overburden on any part of Barker that we mined. This was most heartening, as nearly all the time that we worked we were actually mining. Very little labour was wasted on preparation work. In mining, there are occasions when overburden can be a hundred or more feet deep.

With the long daylight hours, Don was able to accomplish a lot

Don and Gwen at overnight camp undertree.

Don and Gwen on the John Deere at Barker Creek.

each day. In this area everything was going well and it pleased everyone. It made up for the poor meals due to the restricted cooking facilities. It continued to rain every day. We found the air chilly, and while there, we were permanently damp. We wanted to finish the necessary work and leave as quickly as possible.

The tarp we were sleeping under had developed holes. Rain leaked through, and it was impossible to get out of the way of all the drips. Yukon summers were supposed to be sunny and warm but something was amiss this year. We were definitely not prepared for this weather. We knew all the rain would have swollen the creeks, making it impossible to take the bulldozer back to Scroggie. We could no longer remain here to do extra work. We didn't have enough food, fuel or other supplies for a lengthy stay. It was once again decision time.

We had two options: we could call for a helicopter to come in, pick us up and take us back to Scroggie, or we could take a minimum of supplies and walk back. Everything was so problematic. Leaving the bulldozer meant that we would not have a chance of finding gold and earning money. To call the helicopter would cost about $1000. We decided that we would save that by walking out.

I managed a sponge bath of sorts, and donned clean clothes for the trip out. At last the sun was shining, and we had high hopes of reaching Scroggie camp that night. After this past week, it would seem like a luxury hotel. We wanted to take only the bare essentials. We limited ourselves to two guns, an axe, the radio, a couple of pots, light sleeping bags, and food for a couple of days. We decided to leave the chain saw, extra clothing, heavy sleeping bags, tarp and coolers attached to the bulldozer. We would retrieve them the following spring.

Just prior to leaving, we radioed Ursula. We told her that we were going to have to walk out. If she didn't hear from us within five days she was to contact a helicopter to come and look for us. She promised this would be done.

Everything seemed secured. Extra groceries were thrown in the fire, sandwiches were made, and each of us picked up our designated load.

Gwen at a steam boiler from the old days.

Gwen crossing Scroggie Creek on the tree Don had felled..

CHAPTER 9

Twenty-five Miles of Muskeg

We began our hike at 9 a.m. What a miserable 25 miles it turned out to be. The bushes were still wet. The muskeg felt like a luxurious carpet except for the unevenness brought about by the head-size hummocks everywhere. They stood like pillars, perhaps a foot high, with long grass growing on the top like a little thatched roof covering. They were unsteady and only sometimes wide enough to step on; the width was deceiving, as the grass on top made it impossible to determine their exact width. People had broken legs falling off them. Alongside these hummocks were holes filled with water and black mud. Because of all the rain that had fallen, the ground was sodden.

None of us had dry feet within five minutes of leaving Barker camp. We had to use the hummocks as stepping stones. They wiggled and wobbled underfoot, so it was no easy task going from one to the next. I was the first to lose my footing. I slipped into a deep hole of black, smelly muck. I was wet right up to my hips, in pain – two days later I discovered several nasty bruises – and very angry. My red pants were now black. But there was no stopping, no quitting.

We were already wet, so any time we came to a stream, providing it wasn't too deep, we would wade through it. This helped to wash off the black muck we were all acquiring from our slips into the holes.

The loads we were carrying made walking extremely awkward for the lot of us. Don and Shawn each had a packboard with a 40-pound load, including a pistol, a shotgun, three cooking pots, a coffee pot and a frying pan. I was carrying a large bucket, food and supplies. My load amounted to about 25 pounds.

My intention had been to let only one of the pots we brought get blackened by the campfire. This turned out to be quite laughable, as everything that got anywhere near the fire soon wore a sooty mask.

We slogged along in these muskeg areas, making very poor time. We managed a little better on the higher sections of ground. We hadn't brought any liquor with us to Barker, but we did have a bottle of Scotch and a dozen beer back at Scroggie. It was obviously on Don's mind.

"Can't wait to get to Scroggie; am I ever going to have a slug of Scotch."

Shawn responded, "And I'm going to hit the beer!"

I wanted nothing more nor less than a hot cup of coffee.

We came to our first major creek crossing. When we had crossed this creek on our way to Barker, there had been about a foot of water in it. Now, from bank to bank, it was full of raging water. Don cut a stick and measured it. It was over six feet deep. He decided to fall a tree across the creek so that we could cross over. It was rather wobbly though. As an extra precaution, he tied a guide rope to another tree, crossed the creek himself, and tied the other end of the rope to a tree across the way. Shawn and I were able to hold on and use it as a guide rope while we crossed.

With all of us safely on the other side, we were pleased to find the rest of the walk to Robin's cabin was on drier, more even ground. When we arrived at the cabin, we found it empty. We learned later that Robin and his gang had gone out ahead of the rain. We had our lunch and quickly got on our way again.

We were now following our cat tracks, but still walking through water and black mud. The mosquitoes were constantly tormenting us in spite of the insect repellent we smeared on every couple of hours. The next five miles took three hours to walk, as we kept sinking into and clambering out of water and mud. We finally came to the old Barker roadhouse. Don figured that with Barker Creek and the others in such a flood stage, we'd need a raft to cross Scroggie. There were old boards with spikes in them on the ground near the roadhouse. Don removed and pocketed the spikes – about 18 of them – in preparation for raft building.

We were at Stewart River when a couple in a canoe passed by and exchanged greetings with us. By this time we were very tired, very wet and very dirty. To pick up our spirits and gain a little strength, we opened canned pears. We ate them out of our cups, along with cookies. We noticed that Don's shoulders were red and sore. They were engraved with the markings from the packboard straps. We folded gloves and placed them between his shoulders and the straps to give him some relief.

Feeling somewhat refreshed, we set out to hike up the poplar ridge to get to Scroggie Creek, three miles away. Walking was much easier now, so we made good time getting to Scroggie. Just as Don had predicted, Scroggie was swollen and churning, with water rushing from one bank to the other. Even with a raft, it would be impossible to cross. There had been no rain for 36 hours, so there was a chance that the water level would drop overnight. We decided to make camp here until morning.

We had left the tarp and big sleeping bags with the bulldozer. This meant we would be sleeping on the ground under a spruce tree. Fortunately it was no longer raining. We found a sheltered spot to make camp, lit a fire and made a one-pot supper along with tea. I encouraged the men to eat more, because that meant my load would be lighter! Don and Shawn's loads had been awkward and heavy. In spite of all our discomforts we realized that Lady Luck really had been with us. If we hadn't gotten to Barker when we did, we would never have made it at all. Weather had been good on the way there, and was sunny again coming out today. This helped to make the air much warmer this evening for our sleep under the stars.

We spread the raincoats and one light sleeping bag on the ground and settled in for the night. We were all so tired that when, shortly after curling up in our beds, Shawn hollered, "Look – there's a bear!" I replied, "Let it eat me. I'm too tired to care." By this time my exhaustion had far surpassed my fear. The bear went away, and if it did come near us in the night, none of us knew it.

We awoke, well-rested, to a shining sun. After lighting a campfire, we ate a breakfast of noodle soup, instant dehydrated vegetables and tea. Any thoughts of choice over the menu had long since disappeared.

Don noticed that the Scroggie water level had dropped considerably. Although it was still flowing rather quickly and wildly, he felt we had a good chance of crossing it on a felled tree. There was but a single tree in sight that was thick enough to walk across, and long enough to reach from one bank to the other. The tree was about 50 feet high and 18 inches in diameter. Now our only worry was Don's luck in falling it.

To ensure that the tree would not be swept downstream when it fell upon the rushing water, Don said he'd have to cut off all the limbs on the side that would hit. He climbed up and accomplished this, and then came down and began chopping. The tree was growing on an angle on the bank, so Don had to do this carefully. If the axe ever slipped from his hand, it would disappear into the creek – what a predicament that would create! To be extra safe, he actually roped the butt of the tree to another tree before striking the final few blows.

The 50-foot trunk groaned and then fell in exactly the place Don wanted it. For a moment, when the raging water caught the tree, it looked like it might go downstream. We held our breath for as long as it took for the movement of the tree to lessen. Don said that we would have to cross quickly. He went first. Shawn followed and I took up the rear. We were able to aid our balance by grabbing, one by one, the branches that Don had left on the upside of the tree.

Voilà! We all made it safely across without tumbling into the raging, swirling water. I had been really nervous crossing that tree, but relished the thought of relaying this story to people, just in case they were unable to picture what an ordeal it was. I quickly pulled my camera from my pocket. I tossed it to Don and started retracing my steps across the tree.

"Hurry, take a picture of me!" I yelled. Don, speechless for a moment, took the picture. By the time I got safely back to where he stood he had once again found his words.

"You damn fool," he said, "don't you realize, if you'd fallen in there, it's unlikely I could have gotten you out?" I don't swim. Guess it was a dumb thing to do – but I did get the snapshot! To this day, Don still can't believe I could have been so foolhardy.

We were now facing the final ten-mile stretch to our Scroggie camp. We found the motorcycle right where we had left it. Don said, "Shawn, why don't you ride the motorcycle with our packs on it, get to camp and put a pot of coffee on for 12 o'clock. Gwen and I will walk, and should be there by then."

With one of the packboards strapped to his back and the other tied to the carrier on the bike, Shawn did as Don suggested, and was soon out of sight. Shawn had taken the pistol with him, but Don had kept his shotgun and axe.

While the two of us walked there was a light shower, and soon after, sunshine again. After what we'd been through, we hardly noticed we were wet – it had become a normal feeling to us by now. What we were aware of was how pleasant the walk had become without the extra loads.

Rain had been heavy on this side of Scroggie since we'd last travelled it. Some of the holes were larger, and our bulldozer tracks were filled with water. By this time our feet were soaked. We figured if that was the only thing we had to complain about, we'd just as soon spend our time being thankful instead. After all, we'd just returned unscathed from what could have been a horrendous trip.

During the walk from Barker Creek we had a chance to observe in detail the earth's surface in the North, including the various mosses, lichen, berries, wildflowers and other vegetation. Mosses were particularly interesting for the variety of colours. In one place we came to a good-sized patch of wild strawberries, stopped to pick and eat some and found them ever so sweet and tasty. We collected a number of berry-laden little branches to continue eating as we walked.

CHAPTER 10

A Grizzly in Camp

Don and I rounded the final bend and could see our Scroggie site across the valley. The camp, and the trail we were on, were at approximately the same level. The deep valley, about a quarter mile wide, lay in between. We were unable to take a short cut through the valley because the creek that lay at the bottom was far too deep. Instead, we had to go to the crossing Don had initially prepared. Shawn certain-

Tent after the attack by a grizzly bear.

End of the season - plane comes in to take us back to cicilization.

ly hadn't been able to cross the creek with the motorcycle. We noticed he'd left it on the side, and made his way across on a tree that had been felled previously.

Looking at the site, Don remarked, "I don't know, but something doesn't seem right about our cookhouse tent. The tarp seems too far back. Maybe there's been a big wind."

Just then we saw Shawn. We exchanged waves, and the next thing we knew he was heading up to meet us. His greeting was, "We've had a visitor – a bear – and he's ripped up the tent and the overhead tarp. Good thing we moved the groceries to the cabin."

What a mess to come back to! The bear had tried to make a doorway in every corner of the tent. It had taken a swipe at, or a bite out of, everything in sight. Dishes and pots were strewn on the floor. Some were broken, others had bite holes in them. The stove was upset, and an insulated water container was chewed. Safflo oil, liquid detergent, bleach, shaving foam, a can of pepper and coffee had been left in the tent. They were now combined in an unusable mess all over the floor.

One humorous moment came when we noticed the frothing shaving foam enveloping the can. We had to wonder what the bear thought when he tasted that! Actually, the only good-tasting things he had gotten hold of were candies and peanuts that had been in a closed tin on the table when we left. The can was now empty on the floor, and no candy or peanuts could be found. What we couldn't figure out was why the bear hadn't bitten into any of the three aerosol cans of insect repellent we'd left near the tent entrance. It was almost as if he could read, and knew that to bite one would not be a healthy move on his part.

As hungry and tired as we were, we knew we had to clean up the mess first. Don and Shawn filled the washtubs with water for me to get started cleaning and restoring some semblance of order. While I was busy washing and rescuing what dishes were left, Shawn and Don disappeared. Little did I know, they were keeping the promise they had made to themselves. Shawn was having a beer, and Don was into the Scotch.

Finally, at 7 p.m., clean-up was complete. I made something to eat and called the men. Shawn came, but not Don. I went to our tent and found him on the bed. Alarmed that he was ill, I knelt down beside

70   *Rivers of Gold*

him. The unmistakably offensive odour of booze told me the tale quickly. This was one of only three times, in over thirty years, that Don was inebriated to the extent that he could scarcely stand up. We'd had such a rough time that I actually felt sorry for him. I took soap and warm water and gave him a sponge bath. Then I put him into clean clothes. Finally, I got him to eat something. I knew that a hefty drink of Scotch was not compatible with an empty stomach and a tired body.

It was nearing bedtime. I served the usual hot chocolate and coffee, and called it a day. Don and I were almost asleep when we heard the noise. We thought Shawn had gone to the cookhouse for something, but then we heard him softly calling, "Don, Don."

We came outside and looked in the direction Shawn was staring.

"I heard a noise," he said. "I looked out and saw the bear hit the washtub. He's headed for the bush. Now we know it's a grizzly."

I was wide awake now. "If there's a grizzly around, I'm not sleeping tonight," I said.

Don said, "Well, I am."

"No you're not!" I maintained. "How could you, when it may come back any time? Let's get tin cans, tie them on a string and put them around the camp area."

Don and Shawn finally did it to appease me, and then we all went back to bed. I still insisted that I was going to stay awake all night – just in case! The next thing I knew, the sun was shining and it was morning. I must have slept after all!

It was early when Don and I arose from our beds – not yet 6 a.m. We decided to let Shawn sleep as long as he could. It had been a hectic trip, and although he hadn't complained at all, we had noticed he was beginning to look quite drawn and hollow-eyed by the final day.

Don and I began talking in earnest about what we should do now. We decided to take a few days to fold up camp, and then call the plane in to pick us up. This would wind up our mining for the year. It had become evident to us that with only one machine and a small crew, we would never be able to work both Scroggie and Barker operations. This coming winter we would have to look for an interested party to operate one of them.

The motorcycle was still on the other side of the swollen Scroggie Creek. It seemed Don was never stuck for a solution, though. He decided to build a raft with two pieces of two-by-four, about six feet long, and two inner tubes. He crossed the creek, got the motorcycle, laid it on its side on the raft and tied a rope to the raft. Don then catapulted the rope to me, on the opposite shore, and told me to pull. The current pulled at the raft, carrying it a short distance downstream, but with me pulling at the rope it was soon safely where we wanted it to be.

Rain fell for most of the day. We dismantled the sluice-box and other equipment and put it all in the storage shed. The following day I did the laundry. It was still raining on and off, and I ended up putting up the clothes and taking them down three times because of showers. Miraculously, they were dry by 9 p.m. Now everything could be left clean.

Our next job was to put everything possible into the cabin. We loaded the metal trunks with towels, bedding and clothes, and packed the dishes, pots and other containers into boxes. The stove was carried to the cabin. Then we dismantled and folded the tents and tarps, and added them to what was now becoming a full cabin. We had to inspect the pumps, hoses and other equipment before storing them for the winter. These were put into the second cabin, which had been sufficiently repaired for storage purposes.

The prearranged plane was now on its way. With mixed emotions we sat at the little Scroggie airstrip awaiting its arrival. Each of us had a suitcase of personal belongings. Don and Shawn were also carrying packboards, Don's guns and the SBX two-way radio.

Trans North had sent in a Cessna 206 fixed-wing plane to get us. The drone of the motor was a welcoming sound to our ears, as we had waited seven hours. By this time we would have loved a coffee and a snack. After landing and looking at our gear, the pilot was concerned he might not be able to carry it all. Also, the continuous rain had made the runway soft, making it more difficult to take off.

We loaded all the gear, climbed in and buckled up. The plane taxied as far as possible down the runway, turned around, and with the motor wide open and roaring, began its takeoff run. There were a few moments when we thought we might run out of airstrip before we got off the ground. We sat tensely in our cramped seats as the plane roared along, clipping off the little willows that had grown up from the infrequent use of this airstrip. Just in time, there was air space between the plane and the ground.

The plane circled and then passed over the Stewart River, the Indian River and then over the divide and on to Dawson. It flew low over caterpillar-like tailings piles, leftovers from gold mining done with large dredges many years ago. On landing, our belongings were quickly transferred from the plane to the pickup truck, which had been left at the airport in the spring.

Before leaving Scroggie, Don had made motel reservations. This was necessary because the end of July is the height of the tourist season in Dawson. A hot shower was in order for each of us. Then we would eat supper at the Eldorado Hotel. This would be the first meal in several months that I hadn't prepared. Next it was early to bed, as the following day would be a long one. We planned to drive from Dawson City to Dease Lake, a distance of approximately 800 miles, mostly on gravel roads.

On the drive to Dease Lake we made only necessary stops for gas, nature calls and snacks. Our accommodation when we arrived was our cabin right at the airport. This cabin had been built a few years earlier for our watchman. He looked after the jade that was flown 50 miles from Cry Lake Mine and stored near the airport until it could be trucked to Langley.

This year, Shawn was going to be the watchman for the rest of the season. Don and I were returning to Langley as quickly as possible. After the jade season, Shawn returned to the Yukon. Except for a phone call or two, it would be several years before we met again.

CHAPTER 11

Encounter With a Wolverine

Once Don and I were home we had to begin channelling our efforts into trucking the jade from Dease Lake Airport. We had to verify weights and numbers of individual jade pieces as tabulated by the mine. Next we had to notify prospective jade customers when the jade would be available for viewing at our place in Langley, and then we had to finalize those sales.

Our Yukon trip became a topic of conversation with many of our customers, who were interested in hearing all about it. When we told one of them that we would not be able to operate both properties by ourselves, he expressed interest in obtaining one of them. Don and I discussed it, and decided that we would prefer to keep the Barker Creek claims. Both creeks produced high-quality gold (a fineness of approximately 90 percent) and Barker was more difficult to reach, but its area was noted for coarser gold. Thus our final decision was made. The Scroggie Creek lease would be sold, and Herman Axel from California was to be the purchaser.

One of the conditions of the sale was that Don and Forrest would take a D5 cat into Scroggie from Pelly Crossing. This would be Herman's first piece of equipment; it would allow him to test and prepare for full-scale operations. Don and Forrest decided that they would do only the one winter trip this year, taking Herman's D5 cat pulling a stoneboat of our supplies for Barker Creek. The caterpillar would be left at Scroggie Creek for Herman, as would the stoneboat (a platform on skids that can be towed over frozen ground) loaded with our supplies. The stoneboat and supplies would be flown over to Barker Creek by helicopter in the spring.

The supplies and Herman's D5 cat were purchased in Langley so all loading could be done at our place in Langley. Forrest was to use his Peterbilt truck and our 40-ton lowbed to transport the D5 cat, stoneboat and supplies from Langley to Pelly Crossing. From this point they would pull the stoneboat and load of supplies with the cat over the same route they had taken with the John Deere, which meant going to Pelly Ranch and then following the trail through the bush to Scroggie Creek.

In mid-February we received an unexpected phone call from Marjorie Bradley. She and Dick were in Vancouver – what a pleasant surprise! We had always hoped one day we would be able to return their hospitality, and it looked like we were going to get the chance. After his stay at Pelly Ranch, Don had told them it would be our pleasure to have them visit, and he hoped they would come. "Remember, there's an open invitation to stay with us," he had told them.

When Don got off the phone with Marjorie he told me that they had decided to take up his offer and he was going now to pick them up. I had just been released from the hospital after having major surgery, so Don figured I wouldn't be able to withstand the 40-mile trip. However, I was determined to go. So with me placed among some soft pillows, off we went.

Marjorie was a nurse, so she fully understood my limitations. Once back at our residence she pitched in and took over the kitchen duties. Our first evening together with them was spent looking at slides of the North that Don had taken of our mining. We also showed them old 8mm movies of the construction of the Mayo Dam in 1950-51. They were only able to stay for a few days but we knew the kindled friendship would be a lasting one. Besides, it would only be a few weeks before Don and Forrest would be stopping again at Pelly Ranch on their way to Scroggie Creek.

Meanwhile, many purchases were made because anything we could send on this winter trip, including the sluice-box, would save us the expense of flying it in after the mining season began. The bush trail could only be used when the ground was frozen.

A cabin was built on the stoneboat to serve as temporary living accommodations. We also needed to construct a 50-foot sluice-box. Don made trips to several metal-fabricating businesses to determine

Trapped wolverine that Don had to kill.

The wild and lonely land.

how best to make a suitable sluice-box. It would have to be built in short, manageable pieces for transporting purposes. Later, at the mine site, the pieces would be welded together to make the dumping box and the 50-foot run. We would need to buy a welder, air compressor, cutting torch and acetylene and oxygen bottles for up North.

As the previous season had had to be cut short, our planned exploration work at Barker Creek did not get completed and we decided that the following year, 1980, we would spend a minimum on equipment and supplies. We planned to take an extra year for testing if necessary, to determine where on Barker Creek we would commence with mining in earnest. However, we couldn't avoid the expenditure for a Perkins diesel motor fitted with a Hale pump and hoses, capable of pumping sufficient water to wash gravel and extract any gold therein. This unit would give us 1200 gallons per minute at a 100-foot head. We also purchased a smaller pump to pump water 130 feet uphill to our camp.

Our friend Glen Marinello was going to join the crew this year for the mining season beginning in April. During the last six weeks of preparation, he helped to locate some of the materials that would be required, and his knowhow helped us make a decision regarding the compressor that would be used.

Don and Forrest attended an auction and were able to buy a barely used compressor for $1,200. Don also located and purchased new matting for the bottom of the sluice-box. It was $300 per roll – much more expensive than the type of matting we'd previously used, but it was supposed to be much better. At a salvage place, Don had been able to get enough railroad iron to make a grizzly (the rack that prevents the big rocks from going into the sluice-box). Another purchase was for the cookhouse – we decided to get a new 15-cubic-foot propane refrigerator. What a treat that would be! We also purchased a generator for electricity but decided that it would only be used to operate essentials, to keep fuel consumption to a minimum because of the high cost.

One month rolled into another and soon it became time for Don and Forrest to leave on this winter's trip. After their horrific trip in March of 1979, I'm sure many memories were mulling about in their minds. However, neither voiced any great concern – each accepted that this had to be done. Besides, they were better prepared this year to cope with the kind of problems they might face.

They left in Forrest's truck, to which was hooked the lowbed carrying the D5 cat and the stoneboat of supplies. After several days of travel in winter conditions, they decided to make a rest stop. Rolling into Dease Lake late in the evening, they registered at a motel. They opened the door to their room to find a young lady lying on the chester-field, propped up on one elbow. Startled and embarrassed, Don rechecked the room number on his key and it was correct. The lady said her key was also the correct one. They went back to the desk and asked for the proper room key.

"Sorry, boys, the gal does not come with the room!" said the desk clerk. The level of service in some places in the North could surprise us southerners.

The next morning they made an early start, and on their way Don caught sight of a moose. "Look, Forrest," he said, "that poor moose is up to its belly in snow. I hope that's not an indication of what we'll face on the trail in. I'm a little worried, but nothing will surprise me!" With this unpleasant thought in mind they continued on silently as far as Whitehorse, where several duties took up the majority of their day.

They had decided that on this trip they wouldn't leave Forrest's truck and the lowbed at Pelly Crossing. When they left Whitehorse the following morning, they continued on ten miles past Pelly Crossing to the sawmill. By doing this they would cover the ten miles in con-siderably less time than with the cat. They unloaded at the sawmill and motored on at the slow pace of the bulldozer until they reached Pelly Ranch, where by now they were beginning to feel quite at home.

Don and Forrest left Pelly Ranch and soon approached Farm Creek, the one that had caused them so much trouble the previous year. Once again it was bitterly cold and icy, with glacial overflow making travel difficult. Then, when they were clearing an obstruction from their path, calamity hit once again. While they were adjusting the screw arm that levels the blade and changes the blade angle – it broke! Apparently the piece had a previous crack in it and it had decid-ed to give way completely at this creek.

Don swears that there is a jinx on this body of water and that we should rename it Broken Arm Creek. Fortunately, stashed in their load was a portable Miller gas welder. Prepared for emergencies, Don had loaded the welder where it was quite accessible so only a minimum of goods had to be unloaded to reach it. Forrest did the welding repair and soon they were on the trail again.

Under a light covering of snow, snowmobile tracks could be seen. This led Don and Forrest to believe that Peter Isaac, the trapper, was ahead of them. Eventually they came upon one of the traps and noticed a live lynx in it. They stopped and wondered what they should do. Don didn't want to leave the animal in the trap. First of all, it would suffer. Second, if it froze and died, other hungry animals would soon come along and ruin the skin. At this time lynx furs were expensive and Don knew that the trapper relied on the furs for his livelihood. Figuring that Peter was ahead and would have to come back over the same trail, Don killed the animal and took it with them, expecting to give it to Peter when they encountered him. Little did Don and Forrest know what was in store for them.

As they proceeded over the next few days, they continued to find more and more live animals in the traps. Don figured he had no alternative but to follow his plan. They continued to kill the animals, adding each one to their load, hoping they'd soon see Peter and be able to hand the gathered carcasses over to him. They were beginning to have doubts, though, about whether the trapper was ahead of them.

"An idea just crossed my mind," Don said to Forrest. "What if the trapper is behind us, and is coming in and finding all the activity around the traps but no animals in them? He'll think we're robbing his traps."

This thought caused both men concern, but by now it was too late to change the course of action they'd decided upon. At this point they already had six lynx carcasses, and they didn't know that the next trap was holding one of the most vicious animals nature has produced.

As they proceeded, they kept a lookout for activity in the sparse scattering of trees alongside the trail. Suddenly, about twenty feet in, Don noticed that the snow had been torn up by an animal. No lynx in the trap this time – it was a wolverine! This animal is simply not one to mess around with. Wolverines are extremely fierce and dangerous – especially when cornered or trapped. The largest and strongest of the American weasel family, wolverines are about three feet long, and man has nicknamed this animal "skunk bear" because of its strong odour and ferocious disposition. Wolverines are fearless and can kill animals as large as deer. With their strong teeth and claws they ruthlessly attack and tear their prey apart. Although trappers like wolverines for their fur, they loathe the animal for many other reasons. It robs their traps, and when it manages to get into their cabins, often through chimneys, it totally demolishes them.

Don and Forrest looked at the snarling wolverine. It was glaring at them, teeth bared.

"Shoot the son of a bitch!" Forrest shouted.

"It's not our animal," Don reasoned, "and if I shoot it I'll put a hole in its hide."

Instead, he decided he would try to kill it by knocking it between the eyes. He got out a steel rod an inch in diameter and six feet long, with one sharp, pointed end, normally used for testing ice.

The movements of the animal made it very difficult to know when to strike the blow. Forrest happened to move, capturing the wolverine's attention. This gave Don his opportunity. He had to swing more than once. Don said later it was terrifying. He stood on the animal's chest to prevent air from coming into its lungs. He wanted to make damn sure it was dead, he said. After several minutes, he could see it was lifeless. Don now released the wolverine from the trap and found, to his horror, that only one claw on its hind foot was holding this wild animal. Had it given way, Don could have been torn to pieces!

At this point, many readers may be thinking that trapping is cruel, and no animal should be subjected to this form of death. At the time of this incident, leg-hold traps were legal. However, today a totally different set of rules regulates trapping. One of these requires the use of conibear traps, which kill instantly. Trapping has been a way of life for many in the North, and carried out the modern way with the newly devised traps, it is no longer cruel. Actually, when we consider how nature itself works, that seems pretty cruel. One animal preys on another, devouring it bite by bite while it squeals and awaits its death.

The wolverine was the last animal Don and Forrest collected. Eventually, when they still didn't come upon Peter Isaac, they had to conclude that he was not, as they had previously assumed, in front of them. They learned much later that because of illness the trapper had been unable to make his regular rounds. In the meantime, Forrest and Don had to take responsibility for the return of all the animals they had accumulated. It was going to be quite an unpleasant experience for the two of them.

The sun was setting when the men finally arrived at the cabin – a welcome sight.

"Compared to last year's trip, this has been a piece of cake," Don said. "Let's unpack, get the fire lit and put our feet up and rest a bit."

"And one more thing," replied Forrest. "We'll have a good meal tonight."

"That will be after a good hot wash," said Don, "so I can get this wolverine smell off me!" This plan completed, the two turned in for a good night's sleep.

They awoke to a clear morning, the temperature barely freezing. They set up their radiophone and contacted the helicopter base to arrange to be picked up later in the day. This would give them time to have a good breakfast, organize the cabin, tarp the load they were leaving and check all the equipment. On top of this, they had to consider the animals they had collected for the trapper. They decided to put each animal in a gunny sack, hoping that in some way they would be able to take the animals with them in the helicopter and then hand them over to Peter. They weren't sure whether this was legal or even possible, but they were determined to try.

The helicopter arrived about 3 p.m. When Don began explaining their predicament, the pilot was far from thrilled about taking the animals with him. However, no one could find an alternative solution. Forrest sat in front with the pilot, and Don got stuffed in among the animal carcasses in the back seat. In the enclosed helicopter the smell from the wolverine became very pronounced. Don likened the odour to skunk mixed with rotten fish. And he would know, for the open weave of the sack wedged between his feet allowed the stench to permeate the air all around him.

It wasn't as quick a helicopter ride as they would have wished for, because Don felt it was necessary to go over to Barker Creek so that he could check on the John Deere we had left there the previous summer. The helicopter circled over Barker Creek, and a little bump in the snow turned out to be the John Deere. On landing they were happy to find everything exactly as it had been left. So, within moments, they were back in the stinky helicopter and headed for Pelly Ranch. It was a good thing the flight there was less than half an hour. All Don and Forrest could think about was how relieved the poor pilot would be to get rid of this cargo! They wondered later what he did to deodorize the helicopter.

On arrival at Pelly Ranch, the animals were hung in a shed for the trapper. Don, Forrest and the pilot enjoyed a visit, coffee and a snack with the Bradleys. They then returned to the chopper, and the pilot dropped Don and Forrest off at the sawmill where they had left Forrest's truck. From here the two men drove on to Carmacks, where they stayed the night. They continued on to Whitehorse to tend to business the next day, and then followed through to Dease Lake. Here it was extremely cold the night they arrived. In the morning, they found that something had pulled the extension cord out of the truck's block heater overnight. It took three hours to get the truck started in the morning. They got as far as Prince George that day and then happily arrived in Langley the following day. Another trip successfully completed.

CHAPTER 12

Moving Camp to Barker Creek

Planning began immediately for the next trip, as it was to take place a mere six weeks from the time Forrest and Don arrived back home. First on the list was to secure a legal contract between Herman and ourselves regarding the sale of the Scroggie lease. The lawyers drew up the contract, which both parties signed. The contract included a clause stating that the lease would be turned into claims. We were to be paid approximately 50 percent by August 1, 1980 and the balance in August 1981. If for any reason Herman defaulted, the claims would be returned to our name, assessment work done and recorded, and the property would be free of debt. Everything seemed to be spelled out satisfactorily – or so we thought. We had no idea of the expense and heartache that was in store for us!

This year two new bodies were going to join our Yukon crew. Our conversations about the Yukon trips had aroused the interest of both Robert Dubé and Glen Marinello. We had known Glen for years, as his mother and I had grown up together. He loved the outdoors, and the fact that he was a good welder with extensive mechanical abilities would come in handy. We were a little more concerned about taking Robert, a jade carver, who worked exclusively for us.

"Robert, what do you do besides carve?" Don asked him.

"Well," said Robert, "I worked with a chef in Montreal. I can cook and I make great crepes."

"Sounds great," Don replied. "I'm sure Gwen will enjoy the time off."

So it was decided that I would stay in Langley, and Robert would take my place. This year the Barker Creek Kitchen was in for a real treat!

Ploughing snow on the old stagecoach trail.

Piles of supplies brought in by helicopter for Barker camp.

Brian and Glen.

Rivers of Gold

The arrangement was for Don and Forrest to drive up to Dawson and then fly in to Scroggie. Brian, Robert and Glen would fly to Dawson, and then fly on to Scroggie shortly after. When the five were united at Scroggie they would all become involved in the moving of equipment and supplies from there to Barker Creek, where the mining would be taking place this year.

Don and Forrest set off for Dawson on what had now become a familiar route. This trip would have been much the same as any of their previous ones, except for one humorous incident. It was quite late in the evening as they were nearing Smithers on Highway 16, and they still hadn't eaten supper.

"I know a place we can get a bite to eat," Forrest said, "and I'll make a call home." They drove in and parked. Forrest headed for a phone, while Don sat in the truck waiting for him to finish his call before they went in to eat. Don could hardly believe his eyes when the glass doors of the hotel's restaurant opened and what appeared to be a naked lady walked by the phone booth and then past the truck.

Don thought, "Gee I don't know if this old grandpa should be going into this place."

When Forrest finished his call and came back to get him, Don said, "Forrest, is that why you stop here?"

It became obvious, however, that both Forrest and the restaurant were innocent parties to the unexplainable incident. Forrest had not even seen the lady. He probably would have dropped the phone if he had. It's just slightly possible, Don says many years later, that the woman had been wearing a flesh-coloured body stocking. Being that there was a skiff of snow on the ground and it was freezing outside, she nevertheless presented a strange sight.

"I think you're making it up," said Forrest. But to this day Don swears it's true.

This time they were travelling in Don's three-quarter-ton truck instead of Forrest's Peterbilt. Along with all the supplies they had loaded on, there was a large insulated box that Don had built for keeping things frozen. When the two reached Whitehorse they purchased as much fresh meat as the box would hold, added in the dry ice Don had ordered and sealed the box. It was a novel idea, one they just had to hope would function as anticipated. The answer came fifteen days later, after the insulated box was flown, together with all the other supplies, to Scroggie. They would be pleasantly surprised to find that all their meat had remained solidly frozen.

While in Whitehorse they checked in at the water board and the mining department to be sure that they had all the necessary permits and licenses. At Total North radio communications centre they purchased the SBX radio that would allow them to speak with others throughout the Yukon. They left Whitehorse at 11 a.m. and were in Dawson by 7 p.m., having made only one stop, at the "Cinnamon Bun Strip." Here they consumed tasty, humungous sandwiches and cinnamon buns. Forrest and Don complimented the owner on both the taste and size of the sandwiches. Forrest jokingly said that it was so good that he could eat another. The owner replied, "Boy, if you can eat another you can have it free, but you have to eat it all."

Well, to everyone's disbelief, eat it all Forrest did! He was probably the first person to ever devour two of these. It must have helped that he was only twenty-six years old and six feet, four inches tall.

The next morning they were told that the Otter aircraft they had engaged had developed an oil leak and that the flight would have to be delayed. They got the "all clear" at noon and transferred from the truck to the Otter as many goods as would fit, the rest being left for later. Then Don, Forrest and the pilot took off for Scroggie.

When the Otter landed they unloaded the goods and walked the three miles to camp to get Herman's cat and the trailer in order to transport their stuff, as well as the metal and plywood left there from the previous year, from the airport to the camp. Herman had also engaged the Otter to bring two loads to the airport for him. However, Herman himself was nowhere to be seen.

"Guess we don't have a choice," said Don. "We'll have to take Herman's things into camp, secure some items under tarps, and put his groceries in his cabin." Although they really didn't need another job with the big move that they were already faced with, they went ahead and did it anyway.

On arriving at camp, piles were made of the various goods they'd be taking to Barker Creek. They arranged the piles by weight and by determining in what order they would be required. While waiting for the helicopter to arrive and begin transporting the many piles of goods, they decided to do a few last-minute pannings from last year's diggings. Several showings of gold nuggets made Don exclaim, "Why are we parting with this ground?"

Soon the helicopter arrived, bringing with it Brian, Glen, Robert and the rest of the goods from Dawson. They had made arrangements for this larger, 204 Bell helicopter because of the many heavy pieces – including the stoneboat – that it would have to lift. The contract with Trans North Turbo Air read, "$800 per hour plus fuel."

"Well, okay," thought Don, "we'll just add the cost of fuel to the pilot's bill." It had all seemed pretty clear to Don and Brian – the cost was $800 plus whatever the cost per gallon of JP-4 fuel was. What they didn't realize was that it meant that the customer was to supply this fuel and actually have it ready for the helicopter's return trip when needed.

You can imagine the perplexity when the Bell 204 roared in, the pilot climbed out, glanced casually around the landing site, and asked, "Where's my fuel?"

"Didn't you bring it?" asked Brian, slightly annoyed at the seeming idiocy of the pilot's question.

The pilot's eyes rolled upwards, as if he was praying to the helicopter gods, saying, "Please tell me that these greenhorns haven't screwed this up as bad as I think they have." That day, however, the gods must have been stone deaf.

After the meaning of "plus fuel" was clarified, Brian decided that the pilot certainly had a point. After engaging in a more conciliatory conversation, the pilot confided that he could borrow a few barrels of fuel from the Burian homestead, which was approximately 20 miles away on Stewart Island.

This episode of the helicopter move from Scroggie to Barker illustrated to us that we were still relative neophytes in the North. The meaning of "plus fuel", however, was now indelibly etched into our minds. In the future, our helicopter pad would never be without several barrels of JP-4 fuel.

Herman finally made his way to the Scroggie camp and took charge of the place and his goods. Meanwhile, Don and Robert had gone to Barker with the first load of goods. It was decided that they would take charge at the Barker end, leaving Glen, Brian and Forrest in charge of loading at the Scroggie end. They cleared up the camp-site with the John Deere, which after sitting all winter started up with no problem. What a good machine that was!

As soon as this was completed, Don and Robert began putting up the tents. The whole time they were working, the weather was fantastic. Early spring temperatures were over 80°F. There was a lot of smoke in the air, so the men assumed there must have been forest fires around. Forest fires were a common occurrence, due to lightning strikes or ground fires that smoldered under the surface and would suddenly spring out.

The helicopter loads continued to come in to Barker Creek. While Don on the John Deere began stripping more land, Forrest and Robert did their best to get some order into the chaotic dumping of the loads. The covered stoneboat, which was to be used as a temporary cook-house, had come in now. After getting it ready, they put in the fridge and started it up. Then they filled it with the food from the homemade box, which was, thanks to Don's ingenious idea, still frozen.

At Scroggie there was a pile of light six-inch metal pipe which Don had decided to have brought to Barker to use for a water line. He thought he had secured it well by running a rope through every piece of pipe and then putting a rope around the entire bundle. When the helicopter made the trip with this load, Don realized that he was mistaken about the effectiveness of this strategy. Somehow the rope going around the bundle broke, but the rope that went through every pipe held fast. What ensued was a strange sight to see!

The pipes, still attached to one another, were strung out in a single line in the air. It resembled a long kite tail of at least 300 feet. Luckily, the helicopter and the pipe landed without incident. The pilot could have chosen to dump the load, but said he didn't feel it was dangerous as long as he kept well above tree level until landing time.

Brian and Glen arrived at Barker with the last load flown from Scroggie. There were many jobs to keep the men busy. One of the first things they accomplished was building a cabin out of some of the plywood. Don called it the "master cabin." They also put shelving in the cookhouse. It was beginning to look quite organized. They built the privy on a slight incline, about 200 feet from the cookhouse. It had walls but no door or roof. Business was taken care of here under open skies. This was also true of the Yukon shower that they built. Even so, it was serviceable and quite a luxury, given our surroundings.

Everyone's days were very busy, but each had spare time in the evening to do what they pleased. Some of the men used this time to read a book. Brian used his time to plant a garden. Don and Brian love gardening, and knowing how welcome fresh vegetables are in these isolated spots, Brian had brought along seeds and plants from Langley. He had tomato, cabbage, lettuce and parsley plants and seed potatoes. Brian put in the plants first, then the seeds. He even included flowers.

During the day the men all took turns at most of the routine camp work, but each one had to take care of washing their own clothes. Robert, the "chef", was doing all the cooking though. Nothing outstanding had come from this yet, but he was working with improvised conditions so everyone was more than patient regarding the meals they were getting.

Transforming the lease into mining claims was another thing the men had to accomplish. In total they finished the first fourteen claims and then staked one lease up Dixie Creek, and one at a right angle to it. Once leases were recorded in the Dawson mining office, we would have use of that ground for mining purposes.

The stripping was progressing well too. A road was made down the hill to the pump station and the sump was made for the pump at this location. Al Rothwell of the Yukon Government Water Board came and inspected the operation. He gave a few suggestions for controlling the sluicing water after it had washed the gravel in the sluice-box and made its way to the settling ponds prior to re-entering the creek.

The settling pond was being built, but was not yet completed. Brian got into a wetsuit to go into it; the water in Barker Creek was icy cold. He was throwing out rocks to deepen the water for the suction hose. When he got to the finer gravel, Don and he decided to pan a few shovelfuls. To their delight, there were nuggets. They found some small ones, and one the size of a finger nail.

The leaves, showing signs of spring, were popping out on the trees in the surrounding hills. The fresh green was like a new dress, and brought an end to the winter blahs. Constant daylight was pleasant. So pleasant, in fact, that they often found themselves still hard at work at 11 p.m.

The camp was on an old dry river bed, now a bench, about 130 feet above the present Barker Creek. A small pump and hose pumped the water uphill for camp use. There was usually a slight breeze on the bench, which saved the men from being bothered by the mosquitoes. This was not the case down in the creek bottom. Here every footstep brought a cloud of mosquitoes buzzing and flying about.

While rummaging through the derelict old cabin with its sunken roof, crumbling walls and dirt floor, Don found a wooden butter box with "Barrhead Creamery" printed on it. Barrhead is in Alberta. It is the nearest town to the place Don was born. Don decided to keep that box, and to this day it remains in his possession.

One morning early, Don was up before breakfast. He was under the assumption that he was the only one up until he happened to glance toward the outhouse in time to see the roll of toilet paper go flying down the hill. Out loud he said, "Who in hell is doing such a crazy thing?"

No sooner were the words out of his mouth when the guilty party, a big black bear, appeared coming out of the privy. From a safe distance Don hollered, "That wasn't built for you. You've got the wrong idea about toilet paper, and it's obvious it would be impossible for you to sit on the seat." It was almost as if the bear got the message, because he then ambled off toward the creek. For the most part, bears caused no problems.

The men were now constructing the second cabin, which was to house two or three employees. The tents were gradually being eliminated for these more durable and pleasant accommodations. They even had airtight heaters for each cabin this year. These little wood-burning heaters provided quick heat when one had dry kindling and dry wood.

The weather at the camp continued fair. There had been no rain for several weeks. This was immensely helpful in getting the camp in order and the mining operation started. In fact, lots of work was getting done. Don made a stoneboat to mount the sluice-box on and Glen welded the sections of the sluice-box together. The pump for sluicing was mounted on skids above the sump across the creek. It was mounted at least six feet above the water level on that particular day, to allow for higher water. A fish screen was installed over the suction-hose intake. This would prevent fish from being sucked into the pump and dying. Glen and Brian marked and cut a line to increase the number of our leases.

Once when the helicopter pilot came, Don sent a letter with him to mail in Dawson. In it he wrote to me, "Everything is going well in camp, except our 'chef' is not a cook. We have all lost weight. We haven't seen any of those fancy crepes, and little of anything else."

The first morning that things were in some semblance of order, it seemed that a decent breakfast should be a top priority. With a very hearty appetite gnawing at their belts, Forrest, Don, Brian and Glen were punctually seated at the kitchen table eagerly awaiting the first culinary servings of "Chef Robert." Slightly mystified by the apparent absence of the chef, the expectant foursome were relieved to hear his footsteps on the outside stairs of the cookhouse. Their eager smiles froze in place as a wild apparition of fuzzy hair, three days' growth of beard and last week's clothes made a beeline to the kitchen sink.

It's a big no-no to do personal grooming in the kitchen, so all were shocked when Robert proceeded to wash his hands and face and then dry same on the kitchen tea towel. After this violation of house rules, Robert turned to face his now somewhat apprehensive audience and said, "I am ready." (Frequent washing of hands is actually a must when handling food and this was required and expected in camp. We used the same rules as fine dining establishments.)

With a flourish and a great deal of commotion with the pots and pans, the chef started creating the famous crepes. After several attempts, a plate was placed in front of each of the ravenous crew. Imagine their dismay, when all that was evident on each of their plates were little, paper-thin pancakes the size of a silver dollar, smeared with strawberry jam. With slightly sick looks, each hungry man gingerly forked a semi-cooked morsel from plate to mouth. Visions of lean bacon, piles of toast and multiple eggs vanished in an instant. Obviously, there were momentous changes about to occur in the chef's job description.

Brian looked at Robert and said, "Robert, you are returning to Langley when I leave here." Don quickly affirmed Brian's statement. It was evident that someone else would soon be filling the open position of camp cook – namely me!

It was not long after, that the helicopter came to pick up Brian and Robert. Their sojourn in the Yukon was completed – Robert's a little earlier than expected!

Helicopter moving caboose from Scroggie Creek to Barker Creek.

CHAPTER 13

Settling In at Barker Camp

Once back doing his carving in Langley, Robert sheepishly admitted that he'd been a failure in the North. He said he would like to donate some of his labour, sufficient to at least repay the cost of his airfare. We graciously accepted.

Brian was now back in the normal swing of business at Lee's Jade and Opals, and I was busy with both this company and making preparations for travelling north. Don phoned to say that he would fly home to meet my aunt and uncle, who were visiting from Australia. Don and I planned to leave five days after this for Watson Lake, charter a plane to go from there to the Mohawk jade mine near Dease Lake, take stock of the jade production, and do the necessary evaluating of the jade.

This plan went off without a hitch. Satisfied that the jade would be ready for the fall market, we began our journey to Barker Creek to resume our gold mining. We flew back to Watson Lake.

Now I never travel unless I am in dress clothes with all my make-up on. This time I was travelling in a well-cut coral pantsuit and white high-heeled shoes. I had Don dressed in a dashing pale-blue polyester casual suit – the material of the day – and he was looking very smart. Had it been his choice, Don would have travelled in his blue jeans. We were quite a dressed-up couple to be landing in Watson Lake.

I had never been at Watson Lake airport before, but I thought I had read somewhere years earlier that there was a limousine service from the airport to the town – population 1,800. When we arrived, I noticed a young fellow sitting on a bench. He was clad in well-worn clothes and scuffed boots, and had a packboard by his side. Not seeing any sign of a limousine or even a taxi, I went over to him and asked, "Could you please tell me what time the limousine goes to Watson Lake?"

The young man almost choked on his own laughter. He kept bending over, slapping his knees and repeating, "Limousine? Limousine?" He must have been thinking, "Where does this lady come from?" and "Does she have a lot to learn!" Just at that moment a gentleman came over and said he had a car and would be glad to give us a lift. Through his generosity, we were able to get to our motel, where we spent the rest of the day. The next day we flew to Whitehorse.

Meanwhile a friend of ours, Charlie, had contacted Brian in Langley and asked when we would be returning to Barker Creek. Brian told him which day we were going to be in Whitehorse, and Charlie made arrangements to meet us there. During the winter he had expressed a desire to see the gold-mining property and spend time in the North.

At the time we told him he was welcome, but would have to make his own way there. So when Don called Brian from Whitehorse and was told of Charlie's plans, he was concerned. This was not the way it was supposed to be. If Charlie and his gear went in the helicopter there would be no room for groceries – and of course the helicopter trip was on our tab. Helicopter service was so expensive that we had to make full use of all trips. When groceries came in, people or empty propane bottles went out.

We had already contacted Ursula from Langley and asked her to purchase the groceries and have them at the helicopter pad ready to go in with Don and me. These instructions had been carried out. The groceries were waiting when we got off the plane in Dawson City. With Charlie, his gear, Don, myself and the pilot, there was little room left for groceries. If we'd known which box held the perishables we could have taken them and left the rest for another planned trip. Unfortunately we didn't. Consequently, just as we had feared, the helicopter had to make a second trip to Barker later that day.

Don and I were not very pleased. In fact we were feeling pretty angry most of the day. Charlie, however, was a good friend and likely never realized how expensive the helicopter was. He also had no idea of the financial pressures we were under at the time.

This was my first sighting of Barker Creek with camp set up. It looked neat, but my phobia about things that are not colour-coordinated kicked in immediately. I decided that my first spare-time job would be to get the paint brushes out and begin painting all the buildings. This time I decided they would be barn red with white trim. There'd been a special on the barn-red paint!

I decided that it would be interesting to go outdoors and work alongside the men anytime I wasn't busy with the camp cleaning and cooking. Not accustomed to wearing a hat, I went to work bareheaded. The sun was very hot, and in no time at all I was suffering the consequences of this wardrobe omission. Not only did I get a sunburnt scalp, I also got a mild case of sunstroke.

Bills began coming in. The helicopter bill alone was $15,500. Herman should have paid for the Scroggie lease by this date. Don contacted him by radio. Herman said he was going out just then but promised to contact Brian to arrange for payment. Well, he did contact Brian, but did not make any payment.

Our sluice-box was in sections. This was because it had been easier to transport it from Langley this way. It was Glen's job to get all the sections welded together. Sluice-boxes vary in size and length depending on miners' preferences. The box that we dumped gravel into was six feet by eight feet, with flared sides three feet high. It tapered down to a run that was about 16 inches wide with sides 16 inches high, and about 45 feet long. The grizzly was placed over the large section of the box. This was a metal grating that prevented large rocks from entering the sluice-box. Without the grizzly, rocks could jam up later in the narrow run. When a jam develops, the rocks pile up, water spills over the sides and there is a chance of gold being washed over the sides and end.

After Glen had completed putting it together, we had to decide on the elevation of the sluice-box. This was important. The amount of water pumped into it would have to sufficiently wash the rocks and carry them through to the end of the run, where they formed the tailings pile. Also, at least one person had to rake the rocks as they travelled the length of the sluice-box to help avoid any jamming.

To begin sluicing, we had chosen a spot that was near the camp clearing and the garden. After a few hours of sluicing, Don decided to do a test clean-up. Our eyes bugged with surprise, excitement and elation as coarse gold nuggets were picked from the riffles. Well, it was either leave this spot or lose the garden. It wasn't much of a decision – the garden had to go. This ground was too rich to leave if these first hours were any true indication. Later that night we rescued what we could from the garden and transplanted it in a new location.

Forrest did a wonderful job on a second settling pond, putting it at a slightly lower level than the big pond. This worked better and made longer periods of sluicing possible. Around this time Forrest and Don were taking turns doing the stripping. Glen took charge of welding and hard-surfacing corner bits of the bulldozer. The corners continued to get worn down from working in the rock and gravel and were in constant need of rebuilding. Glen did a super job with this.

Eventually we began extending the property, which meant more staking was required. Within one day the job of putting tags on some of the claims was accomplished.

One Sunday we all voted to take the day off. In spite of the rain, each of us decided to leave camp. Forrest and Glen said they were going to hike up Agate Creek and do a little exploring in that direction. Don, Charlie and I decided to walk along Barker and Dixie Creeks. Don said, "I'll take the fishing rod. It will be a nice treat to have fresh fish for supper." We had spotted a few fish in Barker Creek, but on this day none could be tempted with the delectable morsel at the end of Don's hook. We got back to camp at about 4 p.m., and about 6 p.m. in came Glen and Forrest. They'd had a good day but were disappointed at the one thing missing when they got back to camp – the fish dinner they'd been looking forward to!

The starter on the John Deere began giving us problems. We had to call Ursula and arrange for a new one to be sent in. A starter was ordered from Vancouver, and when it arrived in Dawson, Ursula got groceries for us and sent them with the chopper on the same trip.

We were not getting a lot of rain, and the continuing hot, dry weather was lowering the water level in the creek. We decided to take a day off from sluicing and get other jobs done. Don made a lean-to building for storing oil and grease. I did the laundry and baked bread. The rest of the crew built a rack for fire-prevention tools and painted the tools red. In general it became a camp clean-up day. Then Don, Forrest and Glen went down the hill closer to the water where the trees were bigger. With a chain saw, they began cutting down trees. Then they hauled twelve of them back to camp. In the following days they would intermittently cut, and then haul trees back. They were using the logs to build a storage shed for the machinery during the winter.

The hot weather carried on and the water level in the creek continued to drop. We had sufficient water to sluice for only a couple of hours a day. We decided to work on the storage building and make one more settling pond. The wall of one of the ponds broke, but fortunately not enough to cause muddy water to get into the creek. The settling ponds are necessary. Once the sluicing is done and the water is dirty from washing the gravel, the used water must go to a series of ponds to settle out so that the water is clear before it enters the creek again.

The next thing we knew it began to pour rain. It rained and rained and rained – for several days. Now we couldn't do the sluicing because the water was everywhere. It had turned the ground into a potential mudslide. It seemed either there was not enough water or we got a flood – no happy medium for us in this year's weather.

CHAPTER 14

Keeping Our Finds a Secret

Forrest was a good bulldozer operator – he just loved being on the machine. He'd work for hours, happily stripping and pushing the mud to expose the gravel to be sluiced. After this particularly heavy rain, Don said, "Go easy on the stripping today, Forrest, or the mud will become uncontrollable."

Forrest did a little too much and the mudslide started heading in the direction of the camp. We had visions of all our buildings getting wiped out and going over the embankment. Don hurriedly jumped on the John Deere and for hours made diversion ditches to divert the slide from the camp. Some did enter the creek though; it was unavoidable. As if using ESP, the environmental inspector called on us the following day! He ended up writing a favourable report on us, however, as he could see we had shut down our operation, and had done our best to control the situation.

This was far from the only problem we developed. Oil began leaking from hydraulic hoses, and splits appeared in the frame and blade of the bulldozer. We made a phone call to Brian and requested he purchase gaskets and seals from the John Deere dealer and quickly send them to us. In the meantime, Don and Glen repaired the splits as much as possible.

It continued to rain. Puddles and mud were all over the ground. Thankfully, the storage building now had a roof on it. Since there was still tin left over, it was used over the plywood on the cookhouse roof.

We finally received the new gaskets and seals for the John Deere, along with fresh groceries. The repair to the John Deere was completed and sluicing had resumed, as there had been improvement in the weather for a couple of days. The mud was now under control. Once again we were able to use the John Deere to push gravel into the sluice-box. The amount of nuggets we were getting looked promising.

Then the rains came again! Thunder, lightning and a storm that shook the earth came down on us. The winds whipped the air for several hours. This heavy rain kept on all night. Luckily, the cookhouse and cabins stayed warm and dry, and we were pleased to see that not one produced any leaks.

The rain had not given up by morning, so we all went to work in it. We found a leak in the settling pond. It wasn't serious, but it still had to be fixed. We remedied it by deepening the 50,000-square-foot pond by one foot. It was a big job that carried on into the next day.

As the bulldozer was deepening the cut of the gravel seam and the gravel was being put through the sluice-box, Don began to see a pattern of the old riverbed layers. These layers hold the gold just above the bedrock. He was pleased. The sluicing in this area was proving productive. Each night after the water was shut off, the nuggets that were showing in the riffles were picked out with tweezers, weighed and put into a container. With the tweezers we were able to pick out a few five- to six-pennyweight nuggets, and a couple of even larger ones. (There are 20 pennyweight in a troy ounce.) We decided not to leave them in the sluice-box until clean-up in case they got washed away.

In the bottom of the sluice-box was a special type of carpeting, or cocoa mat. Placed over this was a type of grid work, or shallow steps – approximately twenty-four of them – welded up to resemble a horizontal ridged ladder. The larger rocks are quickly washed and carried over this metal. The finer gravel, the black sand and the gold settle in the carpet beneath the metal. The gold is retrieved when the mats are washed at clean-up time.

Every day the crew took time to work on the storage shed. The rows of logs were coming one by one. The logs should have been peeled, but they weren't. Later we would come to regret this omission. We didn't realize until the following year just how much damage this oversight could create. Many piles of sawdust would be found all around the walls and we would literally hear the chomping of the worms inside the logs devouring the building we had worked so hard to construct.

Many other odd jobs got done this year. The toilet now had a roof. The Yukon shower was cosmetically improved, and the helicopter pad was sporting a wind sock. Everything looked good.

The Suzuki 125 motorcycle with wide, knobby tires proved most useful. No one complained about going up and down the 130-foot steep hillside to turn the pump on or off, as all that was required was to jump on the motorcycle, fly down and roar back up.

One such trip sticks out in Don's mind. The heavy rains had made the road to the pump very slippery. In a hurry to get to the pump, Don tried to negotiate the first turn at his usual speed, making no allowances for the slippery conditions. Like greased lightning, the bike went out from under him and he flew over the front of it, while the Suzuki somersaulted over him. Luckily nothing but his pride was injured. He got up, kicked the bike, its motor still running, and after directing some rough words at it, climbed back on and finished his mission.

Torrential rains began to fall again, presenting many problems for all of us. The creek was rising rapidly, and we feared for our water pumps. We could easily move the small pumps used for the camp, but the large one, used for sluicing, caused us real concern. The high water level made it difficult to move around with the bulldozer. If we'd had a crane it would have been simple to lift the pump, but we had limited equipment, and a crane wasn't part of it. At least we had the John Deere with a winch on the back.

A check showed the water lapping at the platform holding the pump. The bulldozer was placed as an anchor with the winch line securing the pump and platform. This would keep the pump from going into the creek, providing the water didn't rise too much more. At this point, all we could do was done. We just had to anxiously wait to see if the water would subside. The water was actually so high that it was running over the banks in many places.

Overnight the water dropped a few inches. There were sighs of relief. We knew the pump was saved, provided the water continued to subside, and it did. The worst that had happened during this episode was that we got behind in our sluicing, and had extra mud clean-up to do, caused by the heavy rain's action on the overburden we'd been stripping.

The heart and soul of our mining operation was this single 450B John Deere bulldozer we owned. It was amazing to me how well it performed. This single machine was doing the stripping. It was removing the mud. It was pushing the gravel into the sluice-box and it was removing the tailings – the sluiced gravel which accumulates at the end of the sluice-box run.

We were generally a pretty even-tempered crew, but one particular incident put Don's temper severely to the test. Charlie was often panning somewhere. There were several gold pans near at hand, with one always at the sluice-box. Don had just put gravel from the riffles into this pan and wanted to test by panning this gravel that had gone through the sluice-box. He panned it down until he could see gold nuggets and fine gold with black sand, and left it with about an inch of water over it. Don should have taken it directly to camp, but instead placed it under the sluice-box platform, intending to take it to camp later.

Charlie came leisurely walking along and with one quick sweeping motion picked up the pan and fired what he thought was only water over the edge of the embankment. Don was aghast.

"Charlie, you've just thrown away my gold!" Charlie didn't seem very concerned and this upset Don even more. There was no chance to recover it from the rocks, trees and earth below. The lesson in this was that if you ever see anything in a gold pan, don't throw it out – dump it in the sluice-box, where any gold in it will eventually be recovered.

A cow moose was spotted several times in the valley below the camp. She seemed to accept the camp's occupants and did not seem at all nervous. Don said there should be a bull with her at this time of the year, but we only saw the cow. We wondered if Moses, the big bull moose we had seen at Scroggie, was on her social list.

Everyone knew their routines and kept busy with mining, machine

Glen observing water flow in the sluice-box at Barker Creek.

maintenance, camp and kitchen requirements. There were always more than enough jobs to do and, at the end of the day, time for a little reading or listening to the radio for relaxation. Don's short-wave radio worked quite well and we were able to get news and music most days.

Weather was now a real mixture of heavy rain, thunderstorms, hot sunshine, gusty winds and, for treats, lovely, full-coloured rainbows. The mixed weather was creating the most colourful rainbows ever seen – often double ones. On occasion the wind was so strong we would have to chase after our shower bucket when it was blown off the shower stall. It seemed each one knew, when winds came up, what station to dash to and what to anchor. Often it was a mad dash to the clothesline to grab almost-dry clothes before the heavy rain would start or the wind would blow them onto the muddy ground. It seemed if clothes were on the line, that was a signal for rain to come. One reward of hanging laundry outdoors, though, was the lovely fresh smell after they dried. The frequent winds softened and fluffed up the clothes; no ironing was ever done.

When a rainbow seemed to fill the valley with its whole spectrum of colour, the question arose, "Is this the lucky rainbow leading to the fabled pot of gold?" The gold at Barker consisted of larger, coarse nuggets but the gold was more spotty. It was not uncommon to pick out single nuggets each weighing an ounce.

We were mining the bench above where an old creek used to flow, and where it meandered and bent when it was a flowing creek was not evident. Therefore we had to mine almost the full width of the bench and thus we were in and out of the gold-bearing channel. When a stretch of the old river bed was worked, nuggets were quite plentiful and in their golden glory lay eye-catchingly in the riffles of the sluice-box.

Then there were the disheartening days when it was apparent that the original channel had taken a bend and now the stripped ground, which had taken weeks to prepare, was from the wrong place. This gravel was put through the sluice-box with very little return. Moods swung from up in the clouds to down in the dumps, depending on how the sluice-box looked at the end of each day.

The property had gold, this was proven, but we needed more

equipment as the returns depended on the quantity of gravel put through the sluice-box. Don wanted to purchase a larger bulldozer complete with a ripper. This year's mining could have been classed just above a good testing program. Everyone agreed that the size, quality and quantity of gold nuggets recovered this year was acceptable and the property was worth further investment in equipment and time.

Forrest, as agent for Lee's Jade and Opals, now staked ground on Iron Creek, and Glen staked on Dixie Creek. They would do the necessary paperwork to record this in the Dawson mining office the next trip out to Dawson.

Glen noticed one day that his hands and one foot were going to sleep. This alarmed Don, so Glen flew to Dawson for a check-up. Don gave him enough money to go all the way to Vancouver if necessary, hoping it was nothing serious. One can't take any chances when one is so isolated. Glen radioed back from Dawson that he had a pinched nerve. Don told him to go to Vancouver and have it checked, and if possible be back in six days. Next morning – pleasant surprise – Glen was back, stating that the pinched nerve was not serious.

When Glen went out to Dawson for his checkup it was decided that Forrest should go at the same time and go home for his mid-season break. He did, and a few days later a phone call came to Barker from daughter Linda and Forrest, asking if it would be okay if Forrest did not return. He had been offered a job that would extend into early winter. Don said, "Forrest, take the job. You'll need it because this mining will wind up in September."

It was time to do the assessment work on the new lease on Dixie Creek. A good big picnic lunch was packed and all went, riding on the John Deere. Don did the stripping, guided by Charlie, Glen and me, who followed an old ditch and some old workings. Periodically a panful was taken to the creek and panned. A few colours showed and the ground seemed worth keeping.

Back at camp, Charlie had taken a position raking rocks to make sure they did not jam up in the sluice-box. I also took a turn at this. Don began teaching Glen to operate the bulldozer, which started having problems with its radiator. Brian was phoned in Langley, a new one ordered, and arrangements made for a helicopter to bring it in.

With the use of the radio, we were constantly in touch with our

Lee's Jade and Opals business. After all, it was essential that each party knew what the other was doing, so that we could process our earnings against our expenditures each month. At Lee's Jade and Opals the phones were private, but out here at the mining site we had the radiophone – anyone listening at the time of our calls could hear our conversation. At Lee's Jade and Opals, we work with all precious and semi-precious stones. From the names of the various stones, we devised a code so we could communicate without our conversations being understood. The miners out in the hills must have thought some of the calls we made were pretty unusual.

We had each stone represent a different dollar amount. For example, garnet equalled $200, sapphire $500, emerald $1,000 and diamond $2,000. If Brian did $4,700 worth of business that week, he'd say, "two diamonds, one sapphire and one garnet – family ring, pin or pendant."

At the mining site we would convert the weight of the nuggets we retrieved to dollar value, and in our call we would relay a defined piece of jewellery with so many diamonds, sapphires, or other stones. In this fashion, Brian knew exactly what the gold production was. This let him know how much money he could count on to pay the bills, as they were all being paid from the Langley location.

Throughout our mining days, many jewellery items were designed and discussed over the phone lines in this manner, none of which were ever created into actual jewellery. In fact, they never went beyond the phone-discussion stage, because they were never meant to. They were merely our unique Lee dialect – one that worked extremely well for us.

Lee's Jade and Opals continued to do good business, and at Barker it was evident that there was gold to be had, as the tests were consistently proving. We were now putting larger quantities of gravel through the sluice-box, and had high hopes of "earning Gold" – our own Olympic medal, so to speak. All seemed to be going well for us so far.

Changes were ongoing at Barker. While the mining continued, we began putting the tailings in position so that eventually we would have an airstrip suitable for a small fixed-wing craft. This would be considerably less expensive than having to call a helicopter for every pickup or delivery.

Our newly located garden was growing rapidly, and it was always

Constructing the log storage shed.

A previous miner and his family's home on Barker Creek.

a cheerful spot to cast our eyes over. The flowers did the best, especially the nasturtiums. They enabled us to have a few colourful, fresh garden arrangements to dress up the dining table. A few leaves of lettuce and two small tomatoes actually ripened enough to be added to a salad. We planned to do a bigger, better garden next year.

On August 5th Don found a thin sheet of ice on one of the water barrels. Our water barrel was a 45-gallon drum placed on a stand higher than the cookhouse so water could come by gravity and be had by the turn of a tap. This showed how cold it could be overnight already in August in the area where we had our claims. Ice in the sluice-box prevents proper sluicing, as frozen water in the riffles meant that gold couldn't settle there. It would likely be carried over the end of the sluice-box run and into the tailings pond – in other words, lost.

It wasn't often that we got visitors here, so if the chopper landed, we temporarily quit working. One day we got two visitors. The men, a mining inspector and his assistant, were here to check safety precautions. After their rounds, we were given the okay on everything. They joined us for coffee, a snack and a little chinwag. It wasn't long before they were off again, and we were back at work.

Autumn was approaching, as the ice in the water barrel foretold. We were beginning to see Canada geese flying south in their customary V-shape. Sandhill cranes and trumpeter swans were joining the procession as well. The leaves were changing colour on the stands of birch and aspen across the valley, causing the hillsides to take on a golden appearance. Mornings now regularly had a nip of frost in them and the glaze of ice in the sluice-box riffles became a regular occurrence. Soon the sluicing would have to be delayed until about 11 a.m. every day.

During a Yukon shower we became quite chilly now. Having no alternative but to use it, we had to quickly finish, then pop into the cabin where the airtight heaters threw a welcome heat. Since we didn't keep a fire going all night, we awoke to the bite of the morning temperatures. Although this luxury wasn't permitted, the temptation to snuggle further into our warm beds was always present. However, there was still too much work to be done.

Forrest had departed camp, and Charlie was about to follow. I decided that I would go out with Charlie. Everyone's thoughts seemed to be with the southbound birds. These desires notwithstanding, Don and Glen had no choice but to remain at camp for two more weeks to complete the work. Taking pity on them, I decided to make meals ahead of time and freeze them. This way, I was assured that they would have proper meals without having to put too much effort into making them. The cookhouse sure was a busy place before my southward migration. They could look forward to a variety of stews, soups and casseroles. The remaining steaks they could cook for themselves.

Labour Day weekend had just passed. Around this time many of the shops and hotels in Dawson would be buttoning up for the season. Our remaining time would be taken preparing and storing equipment for the winter for our camp season's close.

Glen said, "Well, I have now seen all seasons in the Yukon." He was right. He had made the winter trip with Don, returned to work in the spring, continued for the summer, and now autumn had arrived. We woke up September 2nd to find a light fall of snow. This blanket of snow gave the camp an appealing, pristine look. Unfortunately, it didn't last long. We were making many trips in and out of the cabins while packing goods to either store or take with us. When the sun began peeping through, we soon had wet mud globbing onto our boots as we trekked back and forth.

With the evening temperatures dropping, it became too cold to sit outside. This time of year brought other pleasures we could take advantage of, though. It was daylight until after 10 p.m., so it was light enough to read with the sunlight alone. There was also the wonderment of the aurora borealis, revealing curtains of shimmering, coloured lights. They danced in ribbons, swishing across the northern sky. Some people say that the aurora borealis, better known as the northern lights, are silent. But each of us, while at Barker Creek, heard the swishing noises. The night sky was in motion. It was an amazing, spell-casting phenomenon. The most dominant colour was green, but gold, blue and mauve also intermingled, presenting the appearance of a ribbon-candy stairway leading to the heavens. To see this only once is worth a trip to these parts.

We were kept busy winterizing the camp. One cabin was left unlocked in case anyone who passed by was in need. Inside we left dried foods – including rice, spaghetti, noodle soup, Jell-O, powdered milk, pancake flour, cocoa, coffee, tea, sugar, matches and other food essentials – in a large, covered, new plastic garbage barrel. Also left in this cabin was a down-filled sleeping bag, an assortment of men's clothing, a pair of lined boots, cooking utensils and dishes. An adequate quantity of split wood and kindling were left by the heater.

We nailed a note to the outside of the cabin door reading, "Anyone in need of shelter and food is welcome to use this cabin. Take anything you may need with you. Please leave the cabin clean and the door shut when you leave." We didn't really think there would be anyone passing through, but you never know. As it turned out, someone did come to the property, and we were greatly disappointed to find that the anonymous party did abuse our generosity.

In the morning, a lovely sunrise painted the sky. Pale blue showed above the tree line and then it blended into a soft, rosy-orange hue as it widened in the sky. It was followed by a sunny, breezy day. Charlie and I would be leaving the following day. In preparation, I did the final laundry, cooking and cleaning.

The morning of our departure brought disappointment. Ursula phoned to let us know that the chopper was delayed – Dawson was socked in with fog and low clouds; visibility was zero. It was unlikely we would be picked up that day. This meant that our flight reservations to Vancouver would have to be cancelled. I felt like swearing, but I knew it wouldn't do any good. It was just as well I hadn't bothered, because at 11:30 a.m. another phone call came. The clouds were lifting, and the chopper would be in. Charlie and I were going home today after all.

I had to make a brief stop in Dawson City at the office of the Mining Recorder. There I would register the gold, pay a small royalty (22.5 cents/ounce) and have it sealed to take out of the territory. If the chopper arrived when Ursula said it would, I would be able to get this done and still safely make it on time for my flight to Vancouver. The gold, 24 troy ounces in small nuggets, worth about $1000 Canadian per ounce, I carried in my purse in a thick plastic bag, stapled shut. When I got off the plane in Vancouver, it would be taken to a smelter near the airport, and ten days later we'd get a cheque in the mail – it would take care of the immediate bills.

Right on time, the 204 helicopter landed to pick Charlie and me

108   *Rivers of Gold*

up. It brought with it fuel, since we had very little remaining. Don and Glen needed it since they planned on sluicing for part of each day for the next week. Charlie and I said our goodbyes to Don, Glen and Barker Creek, and then we were off.

Don and Glen still had lots of work ahead of them. After their final days of sluicing, they coiled up hoses and dismantled the pumps. They put their final concentrate through the spinner and retrieved the last of the gold. Don took the John Deere and broke the edges of the settling pond so it would slowly drain and dry out through the winter. Next spring he would clean them out and dig them deeper in preparation for another mining season. The sluice-box with its platform was pulled up with the bulldozer and placed by the log storage building.

They were working in alternating rain and snow. Happily, the list of jobs was getting smaller and smaller. Glen cut up the trees that had fallen into the creek and cleaned up the area. Don made a couple of roads to ease next year's work, when it would be necessary to move the sluice-box and pump along as the work progressed. While storing some of the items away, they noticed that the new John Deere radiator was still in the carton. The Bar's Leaks that they had put in the leaking radiator was still holding. However, they decided to put in the new radiator at the same time as they changed hoses and installed the new fan belt.

There were thousands of sandhill cranes flying south now. With four or five inches of snow on the ground, Don said, "Glen, we better soon be joining them. I don't aim to spend a winter here."

Glen quickly agreed, and returned to the bulldozer to get on with stripping overburden. This was a job that could be done in the cold weather, and having it completed would be an advantage when next year's mining commenced. It was a good idea to do a lot of stripping in the fall so that there would immediately be gravel to begin sluicing in the spring. Glen was doing a good job, and really enjoying operating this new toy. Don was happy to see the pile growing ready for next year. With the bulldozer, they also did extra ditching and planned for a third settling pond.

They took down the one remaining tent and stored it in one of the bunkhouses. Small tools were gathered up, and the fridge cleaned and defrosted – it was cold enough to leave things in the cooler chest just outside the door. There was one final job to do. The day was bright and sunny, making it the perfect time to do it. Don and Glen had to walk down to Robin Burian's place to flag a path for the road for their winter trip.

A major decision was made around this time. Based on this year's gold return, we believed that the property warranted the expenditure for a larger caterpillar tractor and a front-end loader. These would be added to the equipment. However, we really could use the extra cash, so Don made some last efforts to contact Herman for the money he owed us. He was informed that Herman had left the Scroggie camp and returned to California.

Don and Glen ordered the helicopter for some time between 10 a.m. and 3 p.m. the following day. Then they finished up the few last-minute jobs. There was a nippy wind blowing, but a cloudless sky, when Rod flew the helicopter in to pick them up. They left Barker camp at 3 p.m. that day.

In the chopper, Don mentally tabulated the results of the year's

Sluicing at our Barker Creek claim.

mining, and was satisfied that the year had been a successful one. When they landed in Dawson, they transferred their belongings to the truck Don had left there in the spring. The two decided to stay overnight in Dawson and make an early start for a warmer climate the next day.

When morning came, they started out on the now familiar journey south from Dawson City, travelling on the Klondike Highway to Whitehorse. The next day they drove the Alcan (Alaska) Highway to the Cassiar Highway and branched off to make the trip to Dease Lake.

For the next two weeks, Don and Glen stayed at the Dease Lake cabin organizing jade shipments. Don had the pilot make more trips per day than usual, flying the jade from the mine 50 miles to Dease Lake airport. He organized trucks to haul the jade to our Langley yard. When the last load of jade left Dease Lake airport, Don and Glen wasted no time in following. They drove as quickly as possible home to Langley.

CHAPTER 15

New Machinery for a New Season

Everyone was now home, enjoying the brisk pace of the fall season in Langley. This happens to be the busiest season for our jewellery and giftware shop. We were glad that Lee's Jade and Opals was a good steady business.

It wasn't long before the Christmas season approached, bringing with it the usual joyous times for us. We spent lots of time shopping, baking, decorating and enjoying the social whirl of parties, concerts and family gatherings. As usual, we all got completely wound up in the wonders of the season.

During the winter we had a phone call from Rod Watt, one of the helicopter pilots. He and the other pilots had taken it upon themselves to take a look at our camp whenever they happened to be flying over it. He informed us that it looked as if the cookhouse door was open. He thought we should know.

Don was grateful to him, for he knew that he had left it padlocked. He asked Rod if he would go to the camp and close the door or, if necessary, repair the door and put a padlock back on it. Don would be going there on the winter trip before the bears were out of hibernation, but his main concern at this time was the rodents. No open-house invitations were meant to be extended to them!

Rod obliged, repaired the door, and phoned to report that it had been broken into. Later in the spring we learned that the break-in had been done by a fellow who had a lease up Barker Creek. He'd had a breakdown while on our claims. Instead of just using the cabin we had left unlocked, he had smashed the lock on the cookhouse, entered and cooked, or rather burnt, some food. He then proceeded to throw the high-quality stainless-steel pot outside in the snow alongside the cookhouse. We felt very let down, knowing that someone had abused our hospitality in such a fashion.

We were to learn later that the same fellow had filed assessment work he was supposed to have done, but didn't. Consequently, a complaint was filed at the Dawson mining office, and the lease was taken from him.

After the 1980 mining season ended, we kept in touch with Herman by frequent phone calls. In January 1981, Herman visited us. He was working on "a deal" in California and told us if it went through, he would pay everything he owed us immediately. This was to include the payment not due until August 1981. Herman asked Don if he would take him to Rosedale in the Fraser Valley to look at a larger sluice-box. Don obliged. Our euphoria over the prospect of a payout was short-lived, however. A few weeks later Herman told us his prospective deal had fallen through.

We reaffirmed our decision to purchase additional equipment for the Barker Creek operation. The most important thing to purchase was a front-end loader. There would be many advantages to having one. It would be speedier than pushing gravel into the sluice-box with the bulldozer. Also, it would be a great time-saver in scooping up the overburden and removing it to expose the gold-bearing gravel. Don had also decided to get a larger cat. It was essential to have a second one.

As wonderful as it had been up to this point, the John Deere was too small to do any great amount of mining.

Thanks to his construction days, Don was highly knowledgable about equipment. This enabled him to select the most efficient equipment that our budget allowed. His choices included a Caterpillar D6 bulldozer and a Caterpillar 930 loader.

The D6 had a ripper tooth on the rear to break up hard earth and a gearmatic winch mounted on top of the ripper. It also had a power angle dozer on the front. The 930 model loader had a two-and-a-half-yard bucket on its articulated front. It came with four-wheel drive and had large, cleated rubber tires that would be ideal for moving quickly. The loader would handle more material, as carrying gravel from the diggings to the sluice-box in its big bucket would be faster than pushing it with a cat blade. Also, since all the gravel would be contained in the loader bucket, there would be less danger of losing gold en route to the sluice-box.

These were both purchased from Finning in Langley, on a lease-to-purchase contract. Both pieces were new and therefore under warranty, so no unforeseen expenses should occur, or so we thought. Don't believe it! Bad luck would find us again when we least expected it.

Another phone call came in from Rod Watt, the helicopter pilot. He said to Don, "I saw a horse on your Barker Creek property."

"Can't be," replied Don. "It must be a moose."

"No, I mean a horse," maintained Rod. "Bring some oats when you come." To our delight, this horse visited us at Barker in the late spring of the year.

As usual, Don looked after the preparations for the mining end, while I took charge of camp comfort requirements. Between the two of us, we planned to send as many supplies as possible in readiness for the oncoming mining season.

I was adamant that there be more conveniences for the cook-house. Another 15-cubic-foot propane refrigerator was ordered, as well as a large 30-inch gas stove, with a full-sized oven. We would have preferred a propane freezer to the refrigerator that was purchased, but were unable to locate one. Instead Don made it into a freezer.

"I'll take out the baffles, turn it as cold as possible and I'm sure it will keep things frozen. It won't last as long as in a real freezer, but we will more than save on the helicopter trips." Incidentally, this worked extremely well. Don is always innovating. Later he had another brainy idea for increasing refrigerator space.

As for the stove, the range was made for natural gas, so it had to be converted to use propane. The strictly utilitarian, no-frills range was ordered from a Langley appliance dealer. There was a delay in its arrival. It came one day before the scheduled trip.

Don picked it up, still in its crate, and rushed 20 miles to the place that was to convert it. Imagine his reaction when he removed it from the crate and found that one corner at the base was badly damaged. It had been pushed to a triangular shape and the stove wouldn't even stand straight. We were dumbfounded. What would we do?

There was only one choice. We had to take our own kitchen range, with self-cleaning oven, rotisserie and all the other frills and rush to get it converted to propane. I didn't want to spend the extra money for another deluxe stove and mine was off to the Yukon. So, in its place the plain-Jane model – after being exchanged – sat in my kitchen for the next fifteen years.

We also bought a Hoover spin-dry electric washer that would run off the generator. No more washing by hand!

Don had another idea for storing bread, fresh fruit and vegetables. He knew that the ground at Barker would have permafrost. Don decided that when he got there, he would turn an olive barrel (approximately ten cubic feet) on its side and bury it in the bank of permafrost with only the lid accessible. The screw-on lid and collar would make it ideal for putting in and taking out items. Then he would place moss over the only part of the barrel not in the permafrost. He hoped this would serve as a back-up refrigerator.

This idea ended up proving itself – it worked perfectly. We were to find out that food would last at least three weeks in it. It was the perfect place to store extra baking I would do and extra vegetables we purchased in each grocery order.

During the winter Don had built another stoneboat, large enough to hold eighty barrels of fuel. Its skids were made of two large logs taken from our Langley property. These were shaped and braced, and with Don's innovative mind, he made a floor and box of several layers of plywood bolted together – no nails. The layers gave it extra strength for the load of fuel it was to carry from Pelly Crossing to Barker Creek. The eighty empty fuel barrels they were taking with them were purchased in Langley. When they reached Pelly Crossing, White Pass Petroleum would meet them with the fuel and fill up the barrels. When the stoneboat arrived at Barker Creek, it could be dismantled and the plywood used for further buildings.

Don had also built a caboose. Like the box, he made this with multiple layers of plywood. It too would be used for additional building at Barker. Bolted to the front of the caboose were a couple of sheets of iron required for an extension to the dumping box, and a spare tire for the loader. Inside the caboose was a double-bottom bunk with a single bunk over, a small airtight heater, a Coleman camp stove, a small cupboard that held dishes and cooking utensils and a fold-down table. On the exterior of the caboose there was a wash stand at the front, and at the rear, a box for a power saw and tools. The tools were easily accessible if required. Every inch of space was utilized.

The caboose would be pulled from Pelly Crossing to Barker with the loader. This caboose was the "bush hotel" for Don, Forrest and Glen – considerably more comfortable than their previous winter-trip accommodations. They were soon to appreciate the extra thought and work that had been applied to their bush hotel.

A Deister table would also be accompanying the men on this journey. This is a vibrating motorized table that separates the various materials in the concentrates according to heaviness. Gold is heaviest and gradually gets separated from all the other materials; it becomes a ribbon of gold easily collected.

Don, Forrest and Glen were making this trip. This expedition would be different from many of the previous ones. Forrest would not be using his Peterbilt truck this time. Instead, we had previously arranged with Arrow Transport to have two transport trucks, with hired drivers, accompany the men. One of these trucks would be pulling our lowbed loaded with the new 930 loader, the fuel sled and whatever else could fit on it. The other Arrow truck would be pulling a second lowbed, which would be carrying the new D6 cat and the caboose. The caboose would not be used until the men got to Pelly Crossing, the starting point of the bush trail.

In order to fit everything onto the two lowbeds, it was necessary to remove the blade from the cat. You already know the kind of experiences Murphy's Law causes us. Removing this blade would give us yet another taste of the saying, "If anything can go wrong, it will." What ended up happening later was unimaginable.

Don, in his three-quarter-ton, four-by-four pickup, was going to follow the transport trucks to Pelly Crossing and then drive – or be pulled when necessary – from there to Barker Creek. This would be the first truck to travel the bush trail, previously used only by bulldozers, from Pelly Crossing to Barker Creek. Don's truck would be loaded with items like tools and the radio.

As each item was loaded and secured on the various trucks, it was ticked off the extensive list. On the load, every little corner was crammed with something. Unknown to Don, I had even stocked art supplies. While on construction, Don and I used to have many indoor hobbies such as lapidary, sculpting and oil painting. Once we began our own business, there simply wasn't enough time for all these personal interests.

I rationalized that this summer, since the camp was already established and there was a large crew, I would get more spare time. I could use this time to indulge in my love of painting. I purchased canvases of various sizes, brushes and fresh oil paints for "the Yukon masterpiece." The only picture that got painted was what nature did, and it's still in the hills today! With the many, many chores at Barker Creek, painting for pleasure never made the To Do lists.

Several neighbours, who had been watching our preparations with interest, were on hand to give farewell waves as the caravan of vehicles pulled out of our yard and headed north.

CHAPTER 16

Winter Trip Disaster

The men were clean and cheerful when they left Langley. They were all counting on a good trip. However, trouble started at Meziadin Junction on the Cassiar Highway when Don was sold diesel fuel with water in it. By the time he had reached the Cassiar and Alaska Highway junction, the truck was running very poorly. It limped into Watson Lake, where all took rooms for the night. In the morning, Don drove the pickup to a garage. The mechanic found an inch of ice in the tanks, which caused lots of trouble!

Don got on the road again and finally caught up to the Arrow trucks 150 miles further on, at Teslin. No more stops were made until they reached Whitehorse in the early evening.

In Whitehorse the temperature was -30°F, so it was necessary to have all vehicles plugged in to electricity to ensure that the engines would start the next morning. They couldn't afford to get a late start or they wouldn't make it to Pelly Crossing at the designated time to meet White Pass. Also, they needed enough time to unload the lowbed prior to having White Pass fill the eighty barrels with fuel.

Before breakfast they all started their truck motors and left them running while they headed for the café. Anyone who travels in the North knows the usual routine of keeping diesel motors running. The men had a good hearty breakfast at the Airport Chalet. They lingered over the hot coffee and every morsel they ate, knowing that, for the next two weeks, they would be making their own meals with restricted food choices and under improvised conditions.

With breakfast out of the way, Don said, "We'd better start the cat engine now and leave it running while we do the last lap of the trip." That would take them about three and a half hours.

Forrest vaulted onto the lowbed and started up the brand-new Caterpillar D6. He didn't notice that the control lever for the blade was in the Lift position. Ordinarily the C-frame and blade would be at ground level and the blade would be attached to the machine. In Lift position, one would immediately see the blade rising. However, to facilitate transporting, the blade had been removed, the C-frame put as high as it would go and the blade pushed underneath it. With the C-frame already at its highest level and the control lever in Lift position, the hydraulic pump would continually pump oil against pressure, causing the pump, the hydraulic oil and everything near it to get hotter and hotter.

The trucks, in convoy formation, started out. After 20 to 30 miles, Don called the others on the CB radio and suggested they all pull over to check the cat and their loads. Don had been following the Arrow trucks. When he pulled up and stopped behind them, he immediately noticed a strange burning smell. It was not the smell of overheated brakes. Next everyone noticed what looked like steam coming from the cat. Don raced to the cat. He saw that the control lever was in the

Brian at the caboose – the men's temporary home on a winter trip.

Lift position, and with a sinking heart called out, "We've just about got a fire here, and for sure there's damage done." He quickly moved the lever to the neutral position. They all stood around waiting for the cat to cool, wondering what to do.

They had two choices. They could return to Whitehorse and take the cat straight to Finning to have any needed repair work done. If it was serious, they would have to dismiss one of the Arrow trucks, and then after the repairs were completed, rehire the truck to complete the journey to Pelly Crossing. The Arrow trucks were already a considerable expense. If they had to keep one on standby, it would be even more costly.

The alternative was to continue on to Pelly Crossing and unload and dismiss the trucks. If they did this they would have to arrange for a Finning mechanic to come to Pelly Crossing, check and assess the damage and do a field-repair job. This would be a less costly arrangement. It was a difficult decision to make, especially having no idea how extensive the damage was. The deciding factor was that they wanted to keep their arrangement with White Pass for the fuel. After a radio call was made for a Finning mechanic to meet them, they headed on to Pelly Crossing.

As the journey continued, Don, Forrest and Glen were very quiet. Each one had a multitude of thoughts and scenarios filling their minds, and sick feelings rolling around in their stomachs. They were all trying to guess how the lever came to be in the Lift position. They figured there was one thing that could have happened. A tarp had been on the cat seat. There was a possibility that the strong winds they had experienced had blown the tarp against the lever.

On arrival at Pelly Crossing, the trucks were unloaded. After a short wait, White Pass arrived with the fuel. There were two tiers of empty barrels. The top tier had to be removed to fill the bottom barrels. Next the top layer of barrels was put back and this tier was filled. In total, it took about three hours. Once this was completed, they made an assessment of the load, and decided that if they wished to make better time on the trail, it should be lightened. They chose to leave some of the barrels and arrange for them to be sent to Dawson City. Later they would have them brought by helicopter to Barker Creek.

The temperature was about -20°F when the Finning mechanic

arrived that afternoon. He made a quick visual inspection. It was bad news. The hydraulic pump had gotten so overheated that the seals were all leaking. There was a good chance that there was internal damage to the bearings, etc. The mechanic returned to Whitehorse, stayed overnight and returned the next morning. He brought with him a parachute, which he would drape over the D6, and brought in a Herman Nelson machine to create and blow hot air to enable him to work. Next he removed the pump and anything else that had gotten overheated, such as O-rings. He took the parts, loaded them in his pickup, and drove with them to the Finning shop in Whitehorse. Here they could evaluate whether the pump was ruined, or could be repaired. Don was to call Finning the following afternoon for an assessment of the damages, and the cost.

It was getting colder out, so the men would be spending very little time outdoors. Don, Forrest and Glen looked at each other, and then at their little caboose. They were going to be in very close quarters, and there was nothing they could do about it. The cramped little caboose was where they would be sleeping and preparing meals.

Another foreseeable problem was starting the loader. They had no electricity available where they were. They decided to take the loader across to Pelly River to the small gas station. There, they could plug it in to ensure that it would start when they were ready to leave.

The next thing they did was chop down trees to make a big bonfire. They placed logs around the fire to give themselves a place to sit. Of course, they had to endure the typical features of an outdoor bonfire in cold weather – freeze your backside and bake your front. Besides keeping them warm, the fire served another purpose. The men used it to melt the snow for tea, coffee and washing up.

In the little caboose was a two-burner stove for cooking. There was also a small airtight heater inside; it was lit towards evening to warm the caboose. It gave some degree of comfort to the men when they had to get into bed. The small, cramped quarters heated quickly. After having even a very small fire, they soon found that whoever was on the top bunk became exceedingly hot, but it wasn't much above freezing for whoever was on the bottom one. However, when the fire died down, which it soon did, it was cold for everyone. Their good down sleeping bags kept them warm, but due to condensation, the exterior of the bags froze to the walls by morning. The temperature was -30°F both outside and in.

"Who's getting up first to light the fire?" asked Don. His breath was a cloud of steam hitting the cold air. When no audible answer to his question came forth, he said to himself, "I guess it's me." He popped out of his sleeping bag, jumped off the top bunk, hit a body on the bottom bunk and jumped into his lined boots on the floor.

Kindling had been precut, so within minutes, paper and kindling were producing welcome flames and the beginnings of warmth. Before any other morning chores were to be taken care of, however, Don had to attend to another matter. Nature was calling. Thus, he was the first to head for the bush and their primitive toilet. The men had made this bush toilet by spiking a log, about chair height, between two trees. The log was their toilet seat. In order to accomplish this feat without any embarrassing mishaps, it necessitated doing a balancing act while keeping their feet and pants well forward. No extra time was spent idling on this throne!

Once this endeavour was completed, Don made a dash back to the caboose, where he had a pan of water warming to wash his hands and face. Glen was the next one to follow this routine. Forrest, though, only performed the face-and-hand-washing portion of this activity. He held off nature's call until after making and eating breakfast. Then he proceeded to walk about a half a mile to the small gas station across the Pelly River, seeking a bathroom with inside comfort. Don and Glen did not let him live this one down for quite some time.

Camp chores were next on the agenda. The men split more wood and then built a big outdoor fire. They were now prepared to face another day. Then, when afternoon rolled around, Don made the designated radio call to Finning to obtain the assessment of the damages on the cat, and the estimated cost of repair. The news turned out to be disastrous: the pump was ruined, a new one was required and they had none in stock. It would have to be ordered, and no certain delivery date could be promised at this time. Don broke the news to Glen and Forrest.

"Well, guys, this is home for an undetermined amount of time. The pump is ruined and one has to be ordered. This is devastating, but we have no alternative and we must make the best of our situation."

The mood at camp was glum; very little was said for the remainder of the day. Don contacted me in Langley and relayed the unpleasant news. I envisioned the expense figures climbing uncontrollably. On this day, I began to wonder why we ever got into mining. It was Friday, February 13th.

Two days later Don arranged for the mechanic to bring 45 gallons of hydraulic oil and everything else necessary to begin the repairs, while waiting for the new pump. The oil had to be changed because it had become overheated. When he arrived, the mechanic immediately began working under the parachute. Forrest, Glen and Don assisted in any way they were able. By the end of the day, nothing more could be done without the pump, so the mechanic returned to Whitehorse. Now the men could do nothing but wait, hoping each day for the arrival of the pump so they could proceed with their trip.

After a couple of days, Dick Bradley appeared. Don had spoken to him on the radio telling him of their plight, asking if it would be possible for Dick to take the overload of fuel to Dawson City for him. Dick had offered to do it soon, and, as always, was true to his word. Forrest proceeded to load fifteen barrels of fuel onto Dick's truck. At least the one thing that could be taken care of was.

Another three monotonous and very cold days passed before Don phoned Finning again. He was informed that the pump would arrive the following day, and it did. The temperature was -47°F when the mechanic arrived with the pump. Under these arduous conditions, he commenced installing the pump. It took all day, but Don, Glen and Forrest were elated nonetheless. Tomorrow they would be back on the trail.

It had been eight glum, worrisome and miserable days they had survived. They had endured the toughest, most uncomfortable living conditions, both inside the caboose and in the cold outdoors. The waiting had seemed endless, and had taken all of their energy for survival. Even so, when one of the others had suggested to Don that they all go and stay at a motel in Whitehorse, he had squelched the idea.

"Someone has to stay here and look after the load, and that will be me. If it's good enough for me, it's good enough for all, and we'll all suffer it out together." Well, they all had, and were damn glad that it was nearly over – or so they thought.

They were wrong. A further delay was inevitable due to another problem with the cat. After the mechanic had left, Don discovered a major oil leak in the hydraulic system. He sent an SOS call pleading for the return of the Finning mechanic. Toward evening the mechanic arrived and started to do the repair. It was completed the following day. The announcement that it was ready to go was great news. They decided to get a decent night's sleep in their now established campground, and start out early the next day.

Back in Langley, I had contacted our insurance agent. Previous to this trip we had purchased insurance on the machines from him. The agent told me that the policy protected against such things as theft and fire, but, because no actual fire had taken place, they would not cover it. This was a stunning blow. I tried to explain to him that there would have been a fire if Don hadn't stopped to inspect the load when he did. He had found the trouble just prior to actual fire. My explaining was to no avail. There was no fire, so no insurance.

The new D6 cat and 930 loader were purchased from Finning, so if the problem had been from faulty parts they would have been responsible for the damages. Arrow had purchased insurance coverage for any mishap in transit. Isn't it ironic that the only area not covered by either insurance policy was the one thing that happened? Who said that if there was no bad luck, there would be no luck at all? That seemed to be the only luck we had.

This episode cost us $10,000 without considering the loss of time. At this point we had no idea that this was not the end of our troubles and costs with this machine. All future costs would be ours, too, because the impending problems would all be the result of the pump's original near-fire incident. These costs would include flying a Finning mechanic out to Barker Creek to repair an oil leak that would eventually develop.

Can you imagine the sinking feeling we were all suffering at this point? Throughout this whole ordeal Don and I had been in constant contact. We were both disheartened and worried by this turn of events, but knew that there was little choice now but for them to go on, mile by mile, to Barker Creek. Under the best of conditions, the winter trip is always filled with hardships. In Don's words, this one was "a bloody disaster."

Don found only one positive thought within this whole catastrophe. He said, "Well, it's a good thing you aren't on this trip. You'd
have lasted about half a day."

You see, I hate the cold. I've always said I'd be a prime candi-
date for hypothermia, because if I get cold I don't want to move. I
know moving helps to stimulate circulation and create warmth, but I
would just as soon stand still, be miserable and let the cold take over.

Unlike me, Don's control, stamina and acceptance of adverse conditions is remarkable. At the time, Don's emotions were so divided that
he wasn't in a very appreciative mood about anything. In retrospect,
however, Don has noted that it was admirable how well both Forrest
and Glen met and responded to the challenges of that trip. Both were
as cheerful as anyone could expect, given the circumstances. Glen took
everything in stride, including the cold weather. Forrest, who detested cold weather, confronted it by adding layer upon layer of clothing
until he took on the appearance of a waddling, roly-poly bear.

CHAPTER 17

The Wild Downhill Ride

The time had finally arrived for the men to leave their makeshift
campground and proceed on their trip. After a hasty breakfast in the
morning, they got the procession in order. The cat, with Forrest driving,
was in the lead so that it could blade out the excess snow when necessary. It was pulling the stoneboat with the barrels of fuel. Don
followed, driving the loader which was pulling the caboose. In the
rear was Glen, driving Don's three-quarter-ton pickup.

After travelling only one mile, hoses blew on the cat and oil flew
in every direction. It seemed there was no end to its trouble. Another dis-
tress radio call was made to Finning, and once again the mechanic made
the trip from Whitehorse to the men. By 7:00 p.m. everything was fixed
and ready to go. However, since it was already dark the men decided to

camp overnight at the sawmill site. The mechanic chose to stay the night with them, and departed for Whitehorse the next morning.

Don, Forrest and Glen headed towards Pelly Ranch. Caribou Pass was tough going, but they reached the ranch by late afternoon. They decided to stay for the night. Once again, it was a treat to accept the hospitality of Dick, Marjorie and Hugh. There was a large heated building at the ranch, and the Bradleys offered to put the loader and cat in it overnight. They would now have no problems starting up the machines in the morning. For the men, it was "a little bit of heaven" to be in the warm house, have a good supper, be in pleasant company and have the assurance of a proper bed to sleep in that night. No wonder it felt to them that the morning came all too early.

After an excellent ranch breakfast, the machines were started, the stoneboats hooked on and it was time to go. They headed across the ranch fields to intercept the stagecoach trail and then proceeded along it. Travelling up Farm Creek, which always gave them trouble, was somewhat less difficult this time. The bigger cat could clear obstacles and snow more easily. Two more days of travelling got the men to Albert Creek.

Albert Creek was the place where the trailer, pulled by the John Deere bulldozer, had dropped through the ice on Don and Forrest's first winter trip. Therefore it wasn't surprising when Forrest piped up with, "Wonder what kind of problem we'll get at the creek this time?" Fortunately, no major problems presented themselves this time. The glacier wasn't as big as on previous trips, and the crossing was made with relative ease.

The four-by-four truck was crawling along behind, and doing just fine. Every time there was a downhill grade, special attention was given to blading the snow off the road because on the trip out the men would be in the pickup and have neither the D6 nor the loader to pull them. What was downhill on the way in would be uphill on the way out. If it snowed before the men returned, it would be more difficult to get out if this extra work wasn't done.

Conversation was limited during the long days because each was on a different machine, and stops were infrequent and as brief as possible. By now the men had a game going, they said later. They were talking aloud, dreaming of home, hot apple pie, and sitting in an easy chair watching a TV program. At the top of the list for all of them, though, was a shower with lots of hot water, sudsy soap, good shampoo and clean clothes to pop into afterwards. Another thing that they had not had taken the opportunity to do was shave. They were now all sporting full beards, and also hair that definitely required a barber's attention. They all liked their beards, however, and for the time being had no desire to be rid of them. After all, beards helped to keep their faces warm. While they were gaining a lot of hair, though, all three were losing weight.

It seemed that Peter Isaac, the owner of the trapline, hadn't been working his line this year – they saw no evidence of traps. Although they encountered one timber wolf and a few rabbits, squirrels and birds, including a great horned owl, animals did not seem as plentiful on this trip as on others. Always there was a whisky-jack following them on the trail. Whenever they stopped for a snack, it came within arm's reach. Whisky-jacks are friendly birds always looking for a handout. Ravens, the scavengers of the North, showed up too. They have the ability to make a variety of vocal calls and sounds. They "talk" a lot to each other while searching for, or after finding, a kill they can feast on. A flock of ravens can materialize amazingly quickly, seemingly out of the blue, when one of their number relays the call of a find. The raven is the representative bird of the Yukon.

The men were now following Walhalla Creek, which would soon merge into Scroggie Creek. On this night, they were going to camp as near as possible to the old Scroggie Roadhouse on the stagecoach trail. Although there were old, partially standing buildings and other ruins scattered along this trail, the roadhouse was one of the main ones.

Another cold snap was upon them. The temperature would dip to -40°F overnight, which necessitated keeping the loader and cat running all night, otherwise they wouldn't start in the morning. The four-by-four, however, was shut off.

At such temperatures the air was so bitingly cold that at all times breathing was done shallowly and faces protected as much as possible. Fortunately no one had suffered frostbite beyond the white patches on the cheeks common to exposure in subzero temperatures.

When it's this cold, the machines pass over the snow, each making their own squeaky, squealing noises – orchestral sounds that travel for miles in the otherwise still, excessively cold air. This sound is not heard when the weather is warmer; it's a phenomenon of the freezing North. With the cold at night comes the sky full of northern lights, dancing and swirling in soft rainbow hues.

In spite of the hardships and the tiredness of the men, they watched in awe this beautiful sight and wondered about the insignificance of man in the larger scheme of things. Then it was time to drag their eyes away and go into the caboose to get what sleep they could to face another hard day tomorrow.

Morning arrived snapping cold, the snow crisp as crackers. The four-by-four refused to turn over. Thankful that they'd left the engines of the D6 and loader running, the men hooked the four-by-four behind the caboose, which was being pulled by the loader. Glen was in the truck and he turned on the key, put it in gear and let out the clutch. All the wheels skidded for about a hundred yards, and then they slowly started to turn. Finally they began turning at regular speed and the engine started.

Nothing was broken on the pickup. This was fortunate, as the men needed it for the trip out. Had they not got the truck started, they would have had to leave it until spring when repair parts and a mechanic could be flown in – perish the thought! Also, we would have had to incur the extra cost of bringing in a helicopter to pick them up. As Don reminded them, hitchhiking prospects were mighty poor in this country! Don was especially pleased. He also needed the truck for use once he was home again. Everything possible was going to be done to make sure the Ford pickup came back out with them.

The men had covered a distance of about five or six miles. Then they came to a place where there was a rock bluff on their right and a bank with Scroggie Creek below on their left. Through the years, rocks had fallen and erosion had taken its toll on the original stagecoach trail, built for horse-drawn traffic. It was now too dangerous and narrow to travel without first doing some cleaning and clearing on it. Forrest was all for going down the bank and travelling on Scroggie Creek, since it was frozen. Don was envisioning an ice breakthrough, accidents and damage.

"We will clean sufficient space and stick to the trail," Don said emphatically. "Scroggie is an extremely dangerous, fast-flowing creek, and ice on such water cannot be trusted."

For the next two hours, Forrest drove the cat and cleared the road. The clearing bared the road and exposed sharp shale rock, which in turn acted as an abrasive to the wooden skids of the fuel stoneboat and the caboose. Travelling on the snow and ice had done relatively no damage, but the skids had been gradually wearing down as the miles were covered. This rough rock was totally different. Each 50 feet of road covered seemed to peel half an inch off the skids. Before they had completed this rough piece of road, each skid was worn down at least three inches. It had been a wise decision to have made such sturdy skids when building the stoneboats. Even so, Don was concerned. He wondered if the skids would hold up for the balance of the trip.

They were now coming to the spot where we had left our motorcycle prior to crossing the Scroggie on our initial John Deere trip to Barker Creek several years ago. The toughest 13 miles was still left to go. Don had to consider their situation. They decided to make camp for the night and discuss options. Across Scroggie, they must go up an exceedingly steep hill. Arriving at no quick conclusion, Don, Forrest and Glen decided to sleep on it and talk about it in the morning.

After completing their morning routine, the proposals from the night before were once again tossed around. One suggestion that was easily agreed upon was lightening the load. Don cleared a helicopter pad, and an area in which to leave some of the barrels of fuel. Later in the spring, it would be necessary to have a helicopter bring these to Barker Creek camp. The big decision became which route to take.

One choice was where the crossing and travel had been done with the John Deere. If they chose this route, though, it would be necessary to build a road uphill. This would expose more dirt and gravel, which would soon demolish the remaining skids as the loads were pulled. For this reason they decided on the alternative route.

To follow this route, Forrest had to go further down the trail with the cat and cross Scroggie Creek to a flat. Here there was a very steep hill, relatively free from any obstruction. They figured if the cat could get up this hill, it would be possible to bring the loads to the bottom of the hill and, with the cat, winch everything up the hill, one unit at a time. This is what they did.

First the big stoneboat, with the remaining fuel barrels on it, was pulled and winched up the hill. Next came the sled with the caboose. This was followed by the loader with the four-by-four hooked on the back. The loader was able to give assistance, even though the wheels were spinning. Each piece had to be taken up the hill in two stages, as the winch line was not long enough to reach the full length of the hill. The cat sat on a bit of a flat only 20 feet wide, about half way up the hill. From here, the cat winched each piece from the bottom, as near this point as possible. There was a large rock that they used as an anchor to hold each piece once it arrived at this point. This enabled the cat to go further uphill, where it could then winch the piece to the top. At the top, the piece was parked, and then the whole episode was repeated with another one, until everything was at the top of the hill.

Next Forrest, driving the cat, went ahead several miles to open a trail over to the old Barker House at the confluence of Barker Creek and Stewart River. Ploughing snow and breaking trail was a continuous job, as the snow now averaged three feet deep. Thankfully, there was respite from the cold. The slightly warming temperatures made travelling more comfortable, though the men worried it might mean more snowfall.

When Forrest returned from clearing the road, the men hitched the big stoneboat with fuel onto the cat. The rest of the procession fell into order and the men were on the road again. When they reached Barker House, an old roadhouse with all the walls still standing, they made camp for the night. As usual they fuelled up, built a big camp fire and Don took on his job of preparing their evening meal.

At this site there were lots of straight trees about 12 to 16 inches in diameter. Don got to thinking about the stoneboat, whose skids were now well-worn and in bad condition. "These trees could add strength to our present skids," he said.

Forrest, Glen and Don decided it was a job best kept for the morning. For now they were all sighing with relief that they were within 12 miles of their final destination. It was a peaceful night spent amidst the timber at the Barker House campsite. Being more closed in than their usual sites, there was a limited view of the sky and its brilliant northern lights.

Morning dawned with a decrease in temperature. It didn't look like any chance of snow. The men began cutting and fashioning the trees that would be strapped to the skids. They were unable to attach them to the outside of the present skids, so they had to be strapped as well as possible to the insides. It wasn't until all this was accomplished that they realized it was all for naught. It wouldn't work very well, because it put the runners closer together and would have caused tipping from side to side. They had to dump the idea of the new skids, and pray that the old, worn ones would hold up for the remainder of the trip.

The men began the next part of the stretch between Barker House and Robin Burian's workings and cabin on the bench. They stuck to the valley below Robin's cabin, as they were able to follow an established trail here. It was tough going, with the worn skids providing very little clearance between the box and the ground. Poor time was made on this stretch, due to the extra work that had to be done on the trail. The men were disappointed that they'd only been able to cover five miles before darkness set in. They would have to make camp for another night and hopefully complete their journey the following day. Little did they know that this expectation would be fulfilled, but not with luck. Unless it happened to be paired with the word "bad" again!

Morning started out as usual. The road was rough and narrow, so Forrest went ahead again to level and widen the road. Glen and Don were in their usual positions with the loader and pickup, moving ahead as the road was made ready for them. Two miles were covered in this fashion, and then Forrest dropped the stoneboat to go ahead and prepare more road. About an hour passed and then Forrest returned with the blade in the air. Glen looked at Don and groaned, "What do you think our problem is now?"

Forrest had stopped because, as he was clearing the trail, a heavy branch sprang up and jillpoked, causing breakage of the fitting that holds the hydraulic hoses for levelling and adjustment of the blade. It was once again conference time. Each voiced ideas to resolve this situation. Don surmised, "If we can hook the return lines together and plug the broken piece, we might be able to operate limitedly. We won't be able to angle or adjust the blade, but it may permit us to continue going with the blade in one position, and we can still raise or lower the blade." Since no one else had a workable idea, they decided to try Don's suggestion.

130

While they were working at repairing the problem, they noticed oil under the machine. On investigating, they found that the oil was spraying from a spot that was difficult to get at. They couldn't find the source of the problem. They were between two and three miles from Barker Creek camp. Did their journey really have to end here? They were so close, and yet so far, from their final destination. In a major discussion, they weighed their alternatives.

They could radio for a Finning mechanic to be brought in by helicopter to do the repairs. This, of course, would necessitate an undetermined wait in the cold weather, and by this time their food supply was getting low. After all, they hadn't expected the journey to take as long as it had. Don, Forrest and Glen were tired, dirty and disgusted. They all felt like they were at the end of their ropes. They just couldn't face another challenge. So when Don said, "I'm so pissed off, we're getting out of here," his alternative met with an affirmative response. "Yes!"

Forrest and Glen on winter trip with 4x4 truck.

Before leaving, they made a helicopter pad. This way, when they returned to start work in two months, the helicopter bringing the mechanic would be able to land there. Glen loaded all the essentials for the trip out into the four-by-four. He put the sleeping bags and extra gas in as well. The men put chains on all four wheels of the truck, and then completed last-minute chores. They put a note on the cat that read, "Damaged, do not start", and after locking up the caboose they were all set to go.

Forrest calculated out loud, "It's three-thirty, and if no difficulties arise, we should be able to cover the 80 miles and reach Pelly Ranch late tonight. Well, with our luck, who knows? But to do this, all we need to do is average about ten miles an hour."

Don, Forrest and Glen piled into the four-by-four and started for home – and didn't that word sound great!

They thought they'd done a pretty good job of clearing the road on the way in; however, travelling it back still seemed to be presenting difficulties. Hidden under a layer of snow was a stump; it had been pulled out on their way in. Now on their way out, they ran over it and it caught in the brake cables and was being dragged along.

"Something is wrong. The truck doesn't have any power, Don," remarked Forrest.

"Yeah, it seems that way," replied Don, "I hope to hell we don't have a breakdown." They stopped to investigate, and found the stump. Once it was dislodged, the men got safely on their way again.

After Barker House and the first few miles were behind them, they turned their attention to the next conceivable difficulty. Ahead lay the big hill they had had to winch everything up on the way in. It was slippery with ice and they were about to head down it. Don, who was driving, warned, "I know we're in for a merry ride, and we're bound to slide. And there's a great possibility of me losing control. I hope we can stay upright. Everyone cross your fingers – and toes too."

As the truck broke over the crest of the hill, Don exclaimed, "Hang on, here goes!" They began sliding. Midway down, at a small flat, they were going sideways. This extra width of flat slowed the truck down slightly, and Don got it somewhat straightened out before the wild downward plunge continued to the bottom. After being turned crisscross, sideways and in every direction but backwards, the rollercoaster ride finally came to an end with all four wheels still on the ground. Three huge sighs of relief could be heard.

"What a hell of a wild ride!" exclaimed Glen.

"Don't want that one again!" shouted Forrest.

"Well, who needs to change their underwear?" quipped Don.

No one admitted to that necessity.

It was dark by the time they came to Scroggie Creek, so the truck headlights were all that was illuminating the way. After crossing without incident, they proceeded onto the stagecoach trail, which they would follow until coming to the boundary of Pelly Ranch. In the glare of their headlights they saw hundreds of rabbits constantly darting across the trail.

On the way in, the cat, loader and truck had pushed the small brush and willows, leaving them partially laid over. Now on the way out, the branches and tops were pointing directly at the truck. Some of the larger ones were posing a problem. One went under the hood, just missed the radiator, and lodged itself behind the motor. The men were relieved because, had it put a hole in the radiator, the truck would have been out of commission.

Once, they just missed going over a bank, but basically the trip went on without incident. Their only complaints were from being cramped, bounced around, tired and hungry. They hadn't eaten since morning, choosing not to stop. Eating just wasn't foremost on their agenda – getting out of this country was!

It was midnight when they came to the crest of the final hill. They saw the lights of Pelly Ranch about two miles away. Was it a mirage, or was it real? As they crossed the final field, they watched as the lights in the house went out, but as the noise of the truck was heard, they soon flooded back on again.

Don, Glen and Forrest were elated as they knocked on the door, to be welcomed by Dick and Marjorie. They could hardly believe what they smelled and saw when they came in. Marjorie had prepared a big hot-salmon dinner. The table was set, awaiting the men's arrival. Surprised, Don inquired, "How the heck did you know we would come tonight? We had no definite time of return when we last saw you."

"Must be ESP," Marjorie answered. "I just had a feeling you would be here tonight."

Cat pulling stoneboat of supplies

Men with winter-trip equipment.

What wonderful friends, and what a wonderful meal. Given their eating habits of late, it was not surprising that Don, Forrest and Glen attacked the scrumptious food like a pack of wolves. After eating, the men gave the Bradleys a rundown on the trip. Following a pleasant conversation, the men enjoyed a restful night in a comfortable, warm room.

Don, Forrest and Glen awoke to the enticing aroma of breakfast cooking. They were soon at the table again, savouring a full ranch breakfast. The scruffy-looking threesome, sporting a month's growth of beard and hair, thanked their hosts once again and continued on their journey. Their first stop would be in Whitehorse, to take care of errands. They decided to leave improving their personal appearance till they get home. A bath, however, when they got to Whitehorse would be welcomed.

In Whitehorse Don paid bills and checked in at the mining department and the department of highways and then, as usual, the night was spent at the Airport Chalet. The following morning, Don went to Finning, explained what had happened with the cat, and arranged to have a mechanic fly in to do the repair before Don's return in the spring. With everything in Whitehorse completed, the men, taking turns driving, headed home. They didn't make another overnight stop until they reached Langley.

Don's birthday is March 16th, and they had arrived home just in time to celebrate it. Our family were all happy to have them safely at home, and the difficult winter trip behind them. It was a perfect time for birthday cake, hats and horns – all things that delighted our grandchildren.

CHAPTER 18

Year Three at Barker Creek

It was April 1981 – time for the third annual spring trip. It had been less than a month since Don, Forrest and Glen had returned home from their last journey north. Glen decided that he would drive his Jeep up this year. Then, when mining season finished, he would do some fall hunting. The timing worked out well for him, because hunting season opened in B.C. right around the time he'd be returning home from Barker Creek. Brian would join the men at Dawson.

As usual, Don, accompanied by Forrest, would drive to Dawson. Brian would fly in and meet them there. From Dawson, the four men would go by helicopter to Barker. Another helicopter would have to be arranged to take in their supplies.

Since the winter trip, it seemed that our conversations were always about mining. During one of these discussions, I decided it would be nice to have our daughter, Linda, and daughter-in-law, Cathy, each with their two children, visit the mine. Linda and Forrest's son Lee was three years old, and daughter Tara was one. Cathy and Brian's son Mike was three and Dave was two. I figured they'd be thrilled to have a helicopter trip and see how the equipment worked and how placer gold mining was actually done. As I'd suspected, this suggestion was met with favourable applause.

Even though the days at Barker were exceedingly busy and tiring, I'd found it could get lonely among the hills and creeks. To have visitors there, especially the grandchildren, was going to be the highlight of the season. I was delighted with the plan. Grandpa Don thought it would be okay, too.

In anticipation of having the grandchildren for a visit, I decided that one of the bunkhouses must have a kid-oriented decor. I purchased nursery-rhyme wallpaper along with children's toys, especially ones duplicating the mining equipment. These were stashed in among the supplies going to Barker.

Since they were now using Don's four-by-four pickup for the trips, Forrest decided to sell his Peterbilt truck. He was now so involved in mining that the truck was just sitting, getting older, depreciating in value and earning nothing.

In the last few days before departure, our time was spent finalizing all the arrangements. Glen was busy with interesting arrangements of his own during this time – he and his girlfriend decided to get married! He asked for no extra time off from us, though, and was ready to go on the date Don set.

The men completed the final loading of Don's truck and Glen's Jeep, and then settled into the vehicles themselves. It was a warm spring morning. The sun was shining, the birds were singing and the shrubs were blooming when the three men pulled out of our Langley yard, Yukon-bound once again. How familiar this route had become to them!

When the men met in Dawson, they purchased the necessary groceries and engaged a helicopter. With the four men, plus all the supplies they had, they would have to make three trips. After loading some of the supplies into the chopper, Don and Forrest hopped in for the first ride. Glen and Brian waited with the remaining supplies. They would go on the next trip out with some of these, and the balance would be brought out to Barker on the last trip. Once everything and everyone was at Barker, the men would spend their first few days getting the supplies put away and the camp in order.

Early in the spring we had received a bill from Finning. We were notified that their mechanic had flown in by helicopter to our disabled cat and completed the repairs. Therefore the D6 cat, supplies and equipment were ready to make the final mile to Barker. Don, Glen and Forrest gave this first priority. The loader acquired a flat tire a quarter of a mile from camp, and within a day was repaired. Except for this problem, everything else went well.

At 3 p.m., after an exceedingly busy day, the four men decided to sit on the folding lawn chairs for a while and just have a discussion. The temperature had jumped to over 80°F, an increase of nearly 20 degrees above the previous day, and they weren't accustomed to this heat. They actually took a picture of themselves relaxing, to prove that they were capable of such an indulgence.

This year there were lots of building plans on the agenda. For one thing a new cookhouse was in order, as we'd found last year's too small. Among the supplies, Don had brought a door and windows for this purpose. He unbolted the stoneboat with the extra layers of plywood that would be used. Once the foundation skids were in place, sheet by sheet the plywood walls went up. Eventually the roof was put on and the exterior was finished. The old cookhouse would now become a bunkhouse.

Furniture also had to be built. Other than the folding lawn chairs, none had been taken to the Yukon. Thus Don constructed a bench running along two walls beneath the corner window. He also made a table, a counter and shelves. The counter sported a sink. Water – cold only – flowed from the overhead water barrel by gravity. A pipe attached to the bottom of the sink drained the water away. When I arrived, I would happily spend the time swinging my paint brush, hanging plastic curtains, and putting the finishing touches on everything. It was definitely never going to be the Ritz Hotel, but for camp living everything was becoming quite convenient.

The first week that Don, Glen, Forrest and Brian were at camp, good weather and hot sunshine continued. In fact, on the whole, other than for a few showers, the weather remained favourable for most of the first month. This certainly helped to keep the jobs running on schedule, and made working outdoors quite pleasant.

One of the leading jobs on the To Do list was stripping. During his time at camp, this was taken care of by Forrest. He enjoyed working the bulldozer, so he gladly took on this job. He started on the upper part of Barker, and then continued stripping in the various areas. He had to strip small sections at a time to ensure a mudslide would not occur. It was difficult to judge how large a spot could be stripped without running the risk of overstripping, which caused overthawing of the permafrost.

Don, Glen and Brian took care of the majority of the other jobs. A great amount of extra work had to be done before sluicing could get started this year. With the new, larger equipment this year, it was necessary to bring other pieces in line. For instance, last year's settling ponds would not be sufficient. At least one larger one would have to be built. We also figured an extension would need to be made to

138

the sluice-box to accommodate the larger loads of gravel dumped into the box for sluicing.

Glen was the welder and mechanic. He was kept busy checking over the equipment. Brian and Don assisted in setting up the pumps, hoses and the sluice-box, though. Most of Don's time was taken up constructing additional buildings with the extra plywood they'd brought in on the winter trip. Brian was in charge of kitchen duty and meals, but once in a while Don lent an able hand, putting his culinary skills to work.

Brian and Don were starting to put gravel through the sluice-box. They were anxious to see what gold they would come up with. However, after a few hours, the pump began giving them trouble and stopped operating. Glen joined them, and all three congregated around the pump and tried to find the problem. They tightened this, and loosened that, in hopes that it would start again. When nothing succeeded, they decided that they'd have to call Vancouver immediately for a new part. After all, no sluicing could be accomplished while the pump was shut down. Thankfully, it was a mere two days later that they received a call from Ursula that it had arrived.

Meanwhile, Robin Burian had been having problems with his cat. He drove it over to our camp, and Glen was easily able to fix it for him. He was pleased that he'd be able to resume work on his claims. Everyone at our camp was happy they'd been able to return the favour Robin had done for us during the time our John Deere had almost gone for a dunk in the creek.

The following day Brian and Glen made a trip to the mining recording office in Dawson. It was necessary for both Brian and Glen to make the trip in order to transfer the Dixie Creek claims from Glen's name to Lee's Jade and Opals Ltd. After Brian affixed our company seal, everything would be official. While they were there, they bought supplies and picked up the repair parts that had been flown in from Vancouver for the big pump.

It may be hard for others to imagine how truly isolated we were in the Yukon wilderness, with the only source of transportation an expensive helicopter and the only source of communication a two-way radio. That radio became more and more precious as the days went by. What often happened is that one day sort of melted right into another, until no one was sure which one it happened to be.

This was the case one evening when Don turned to Brian and said, "What day do you suppose it is?"

After a pensive moment, Brian sheepishly responded, "Isn't it Thursday?"

"Funny," Don replied, "I could have sworn it was Friday."

"Well, I guess we could radio Ursula in Dawson and ask her what day it is. But d'you think anyone listening will laugh and say, 'Listen to those stupid hillbillies – they don't even know what day it is'?" mused Brian.

After pondering the situation, it seemed Brian's idea was the only solution. During mining season, evening radio traffic is quite heavy. Besides miscellaneous activities that are accomplished by radio, many camps are ordering supplies and transportation. Brian and Don were patiently waiting for a break in radio traffic so they could jump in and raise Ursula at her call sign of "555 Dawson."

A brief lull came and just when Brian was about to push the Transmit button, a voice called, "555 Dawson, 555 Dawson. This is Brewster camp."

"Go ahead, Brewster," came the reply.

"Ursula, can you give us a time check, please?" Brewster camp asked.

"Seven forty-five," came the prompt reply.

A few seconds of pregnant silence ensued. Then a voice from Brewster plaintively asked, "Yeah, okay, but what day is that time at?"

"Wednesday, the twelfth," came the amused reply.

Brian looked at Don and said, "Stupid hillbilly!" The two collapsed in gales of laughter.

Our son, Brian, had been in camp just over a month, assisting with the multiple chores that were required to open it up and get the equipment working. It was now nearing the time that Brian would be leaving to come back and take over the shop in Langley. This would allow me to come in and take over the cooking and camp chores. Luckily both Don and Brian, who were taking turns doing these duties, were good cooks. Don makes excellent pancakes. He's also famous for "Barker Creek specials." These are one-pot meals of meat and vegetables, slowly cooked on top of the woodburning heater.

Brian's culinary art is somewhat more refined. He enjoys making dishes that take longer to prepare and that have a higher level of visual appeal when served. Both men's cooking efforts were received with equal appreciation by the other men, since they were always hungry when mealtime arrived, and they were glad they didn't have to prepare their own. They wouldn't dare complain, for they knew the rule in camp: "If you don't like the way a job is done, you take over." This generally meant that jobs were left in the first willing hands that started them. If a complaint was registered, a hasty, ". . . but it's just the way I like it!" would be added to avoid the rule being invoked.

I'd been very busy at the store while Brian had been at camp, and I was looking forward to trading places and leaving for Dawson. Lee's Jade and Opals' fiscal year ends May 31st, so the inventory had to get done. I also had to prepare ahead in other sections, to compensate for the next three-and-a-half months that I'd be away. However, I knew anything that wasn't completed could be done when Brian returned. The staff was also there to give their assistance.

I flew to Dawson, with the usual stopover in Whitehorse as there were no direct flights from Vancouver. Rod met me at the airport with the helicopter, and we flew directly to Barker Creek. Rod gave Brian and me a little time together before returning to Dawson with him. This gave me a chance to bring Brian up to date on shop details and news that hadn't already been relayed over the radiophone by our secret gem code system.

Unexpectedly, Forrest ended up joining Brian on the flight back. Forrest and Linda's little son had become ill and required an operation. Linda also had her year-old daughter to care for, so Don and I decided Forrest should take his mid-season break early. This way, he could be with Linda at the time of Lee's operation. We were very glad this decision was made, as Lee ended up having an allergic reaction to the anaesthetic. Fortunately he recovered, and he was even better than before once his surgery was over.

It happened to be Forrest's twenty-eighth birthday on the day he was leaving camp. Before he and Brian left, we all toasted the occasion. Then Brian and Forrest flew to Dawson, where they spent the night. The next morning they continued on to Vancouver. For Brian, this was the completion of his gold-mining stint for the year.

CHAPTER 19

'Gwen, Don't Spin the Loader Tires'

I had intended on resting for a few days after arriving in camp. Looking at the bare unpainted cookhouse walls that first morning quickly changed that plan. As soon as the breakfast dishes were done, I began pulling all of the cookhouse articles outside and stacking them. Once the cookhouse was bare, out came the paint and wallpaper.

How rewarding it was to look upon the freshly papered and painted room when I was done. I still had other improvements I wanted to make in the future, but this was a good start. I brought all of the articles back inside, put them in their place, and then glanced at the clock. It was time to make Glen and Don their afternoon coffee. After this I began supper preparations. Oven stew was on my menu tonight. To make full use of the oven, I baked walnut squares at the same time. Don and Brian's kitchen skills had not included baking. They might have tried it, had there been any spare time. Instead, it seemed there'd always been more jobs to do than time to do them. So on this night, they got their first home baking since leaving Langley.

One morning I came in to make the morning coffee for everyone. At the same time I decided I'd get the meat out of the freezer for supper. Horrors! The meat was mostly thawed, and the freezer wasn't going.

"Goodness, what's gone wrong now?" I thought. I tore out to tell Don about this catastrophe. He came back with me to the cookhouse, hoping he could solve the problem.

"Why, it's run out of propane. All I have to do is put in a new propane cylinder." What a relief.

After that, the propane supply bottles for the freezer were frequently changed. The balance of the tank contents were connected to the stove. Here, we could quickly tell when the propane ran out and the connecting of another was required. Needless to say, the thawed meat had to be cooked, so I spent the rest of the day with the oven going full blast. There were still ice crystals in some of the meat and nothing got spoiled and wasted.

I did extra baking to finish off that day, and put some of it into the freezer for future enjoyment. I decided to have a smorgasbord supper with the choice of cooked meat and baked goods. It was a rare occasion indeed, to have such a banquet. The freezer was back to normal again by the time supper was over, so I divided the balance of the meat into sizeable meal portions and froze them for future use. These pre-cooked items actually ended up being a great asset on long, busy working days outdoors. On many occasions when we were tired and hungry, we only had to add five-minute rice and open a can of vegetables to be eating within minutes.

Usually meal planning was rather simple, as there was not a huge array of product to choose from. I am quite health-conscious. Making meals with nutritional value was always my biggest concern. I did make sure that they had just enough visual appeal to be appetizing, though. The difficulty was using up leftovers. With the huge expense of bringing in groceries by helicopter it was necessary to "waste not, want not."

This became a sort of challenging game for me. Small quantities of leftovers went into soups, stews and salads. If there was too much for that, yet not enough for a dish on its own, the leftover became a shepherd's pie or casserole. These were adorned with a biscuit or pastry top. The men were astonished at what I could do with leftovers. Mind you, I did have one major plus on my side – mine was the only eating establishment around. There was no possibility of going down the street to find alternatives out here.

Generally I stuck to plain, old-favourite recipes. For me, this brought almost 100-percent success. However, there was one incident when some Boston Brown steamed bread did not even make it to the table. I had made this on several occasions and it always got raves. I would mix it at noon, put it in coffee cans, and then place the cans in the boiling water to steam on top of a heater all afternoon. By suppertime there would be beautiful, brown, hot, aromatic bread. Once the bread began getting cold, it quickly got sliced, placed on the oven rack, and toasted. This crunchy toast was a great snack favourite.

One day, water somehow got into the can, and the fire wasn't hot enough. When it was time to take the bread from the can, I found a wet, mushy mixture, which I quickly put into the garbage can. Glen knew I'd mixed the bread at noon, so just as we began to eat he said, "Where's the fresh bread?"

I was caught! I hadn't intended to mention it, but now I had to admit to a failure. "Well, I had to chuck it. Water got in and it just didn't cook right," I confessed.

Glen replied, quite seriously, "Gee, are you sure we couldn't have eaten it? I was looking forward to it."

The men occasionally offered to help with washing dishes but I always declined their offers. I had my own way of doing them. First they would get rinsed, then washed with hot soapy water, rinsed again and then dried. I ran the cookhouse like a home kitchen. Everything was clean and in place. I used high-quality stainless-steel pots, and favourite cast-iron frying pans.

The cookhouse looked more homey this year – the colour scheme was ivory, yellow and brown. It was wallpapered, and there were plastic curtains on the windows. Bright yellow curtains also concealed the shelves, as there were no cupboards. Don had built a corner bench in our eating nook, below the curtains at the window. It was covered with padded brown naugahyde. The table and counter carried mottled ivory/yellow Arborite and the floor an imitation-marble brown linoleum. The overall effect was of a bright, cheerful and cosy kitchen.

The little nook at the corner window was my favourite reading place. In the evening, after heating the water for everyone's showers and then taking my own, I would relax in this spot. This was how I indulged myself after a hard working day.

One sunny morning we had surprise visitors – the census taker had arrived with the helicopter pilot. We had already registered in Langley so there was no problem. They stayed for a hastily made lunch, and then went quickly on their way again.

Father's Day arrived while we were at camp. Don opened and shared the can of toffees that I'd brought for the occasion. We had wine on the supper table that night, and the meal I made was more carefully prepared than usual. I fried sizzling brown steaks, cooking each one to specified order. I adorned the plates with twisted orange slices topped with parsley, and the meat was accompanied by potatoes, onions and carrots. Usually I did steaks in the oven, along with the other vegetables, and everything was cooked at the same time. Separately it was more time-consuming, but I wanted a special meal for this special occasion.

As my days at camp progressed, I began taking on more than the household chores. One of the things I began taking a turn at was the sluice-box. I raked the rocks to keep them from jamming up, which allowed the water to wash all the gravel thoroughly. On very hot days, a turn at the sluice-box actually held quite an appeal; there was often a spray of water that helped cool us off.

My work boots were yellowy colour leather lace-ups, a pair that my eleven-year-old nephew had used in Boy Scouts and had outgrown. It's pretty obvious the boots were smaller than what the usual miner wore. They were perfect for this outdoor work. Incidentally, I ended up leaving the boots there when we left the mine. The next people on the site must have wondered about such a tiny person working at a mine!

In the place we were working, most of the rocks were an acceptable size to put through the sluice-box, and when they were thoroughly washed by the water, there was no chance of losing any gold. For some reason Don had removed the grizzly, the grate work over the dumping box. If an unusually large rock accidentally got dumped into the box, a chain would be put around it. We would then hook the chain onto the loader and lift it out. However, this took a lot of time and occupied the person on raking duty, and meanwhile the large volume of water kept flowing into the sluice-box, piling the rocks up and creating jams.

Whoever was on sluice-box duty simply lifted out the big rocks if that was possible. I found myself becoming able to lift heavier and heavier rocks. Eventually I lifted some that weighed about 75 pounds. Not bad for someone whose own weight is a mere 106 pounds! It's surprising what a person can do when necessity requires it – not that this wasn't extremely difficult for me.

Through lifting the rocks and often banging into the sluice-box trying to keep my balance, I had my share of bruises before the season's end. In fact, from the waist down, my skin was mottled with shades of purple, blue, red and greeny-yellow. Thinking back, there were probably many cases where I should have used the power of the loader, instead of the power my breakfast Wheaties had given me.

During the time we were mining at Barker Creek, we were also building an airstrip. Don would remove the rocks and gravel that accumulated at the end of the sluice-box after washing and push them with the D6 cat to gradually make a nice, straight, level airstrip. This would enable us to use fixed-wing aircraft to transport people and supplies to and from Barker – much cheaper than using helicopters. We added a bright orange wind sock, on a peeled pole, so that we could always identify the direction the wind was moving in.

While Brian had been at camp, he had taken time again to prepare and plant another garden. He had put even more seeds and plants in this year than last. He also put in a unique dyking system. Water came from a ditch carrying run-off from the thawing permafrost. Little ditches had been made between each row, and a system of little mud dams was built. This enabled us to leave a dam closed if we didn't want the section watered.

This year the garden had been put on ground that had already been mined the year before. This guaranteed that there would be no need to move it again. It contained vegetables such as onions, lettuce, carrots, potatoes and tomato plants. Flowers included were nasturtiums, petunias, asters, cornflowers and cosmos. The garden became a happy diversion for a while each evening. This was when the weeding and watering was done. It was growing beautifully, and had come to look like a little oasis on the otherwise bare, stripped ground. Eventually it blessed us with the most crisp heads of iceberg lettuce we'd ever eaten. Many of the other vegetables also matured sufficiently to grace our dinner table. The pleasure of having a daily floral bouquet to admire didn't go unnoticed either. No crystal vase presented them, but our jam jar served the purpose adequately enough.

Overall, the camp was becoming more and more home-like. This year the bunkhouses even had indoor/outdoor carpeting on the floors. It was certainly much warmer and softer to put our feet on when we jumped out of bed in the morning. The interior walls were painted and papered in light, bright shades, making them a cheerful little hideaway at the end of the day. Even the cans holding the matches for lighting fires were decorated with scraps of colourful carpet.

Regular radiophone and phone calls, to and from Langley, kept our family in touch and informed about business, mining and family matters. This was how we learned of our grandson Lee's anaesthetic complications, and subsequent successful recovery. This latter news brought us all unexplainable joy. Although Forrest was talking of coming back to Barker soon, he would not be bringing his wife Linda or the children, Lee and Tara. The doctor advised them that Lee was not ready for a plane trip yet. I was disappointed, as I had already managed to get one of the bunkhouses fixed up with the children's decor I'd planned. All was not lost yet, though, because Brian's wife Cathy and their two children, Mike and Dave, were still planning on coming. At this time, they were planning on accompanying Forrest on his return.

When Forrest had left Barker, we were one man short. This was when Don decided that it would be a good time for me to learn to drive the new 930 loader. I was not too receptive to the idea. In fact, I was rather in awe at the prospect of driving what I considered to be a "big machine." However, not wanting to be a drag, or delay production, I succumbed to trying it. My lessons were to occur immediately after our morning and afternoon coffee routine.

I apprehensively climbed onto the machine for lesson number one. At my side, Don began instructing me. First he showed me how the bucket was lifted up and put down. Then he made me do it a few times. Next he showed me how to level the bucket on the ground and slowly drive into the gravel bank. This step had to be repeated many times. It takes practice to get the bucket full. Sometimes I would get it only half full, and of course this wasn't very productive. I also had to remember not to drive with the loaded bucket in the air, instead keeping it just above ground. All of this was a lot for my non-mechanical brain to remember, and my lessons weren't even near completion yet.

Meanwhile, when days of fine weather were upon us, I continued the exterior painting. I had finished the three bunkhouses and the cookhouse. Next to come was the little cabin that Don and I resided in. The Deister-table building had already been completed, again in coordinated colours.

The night that Don started up the Deister table for the first time, the lot of us stood watching, fascinated with the process. The motorized table shook the concentrates we'd been collecting, including gold, garnet, hematite, small rocks and black sand that were the results of our sluice-box clean ups. It separated them into neat little rows. This made it easy to gather the gold. We noted that there were also a lot of garnets. These were very pretty, but not of jewellery grade.

The weather was a real mixture of hot sun, rain, wind, light showers and frequent thunder. Regardless of which of these we were contending with, the work continued. The most enjoyable job, which occurred at the end of the day, was looking into the riffles of the sluice-box. This was done as soon as the water had been shut off. Each night Don collected the good-sized gold nuggets from the riffles. The joy we all felt when a number of large ones would appear is indescribable. Quite often we found several nuggets that weighed over one ounce each.

Besides this job, the men spent part of each evening on maintenance work. They checked all the equipment and fuelled up for the following day. While they tended to these things, I had the never-ending jobs of laundry, cooking and baking.

During the daytime hours, my loader lessons continued. Not a day went by that Don couldn't be heard saying, "Don't you spin those tires!"

I lived in dread of the times I committed this no-no. Actually, he had it so ingrained in my mind that seldom did I make this particular error. I knew each action counted. Therefore, every single movement was well thought out to ensure that everything was being done in the correct sequence. My total was now up to thirty non-stop loads. It was becoming quite a natural operation for me. Without a doubt, I had myself a job!

There were always the unexpected breakdowns and malfunctions of the mining equipment that had to be dealt with. When this happened and we couldn't mend the problem ourselves, Brian would be called. He then contacted the required supplier, secured the new part, and then made the necessary arrangements for it to be brought to the mine as soon as possible. In the log machine shed there was a hefty supply of items we had anticipated needing, but we couldn't predict everything.

Camp at Barker Creek.

Aerial view of Barker Creek camp.

At the camp, we had one large roll of turquoise-green paper. It was a foot wide and much heavier than usual writing paper, but this is what we used it for. Whatever length of stationery we needed was torn from the roll. Our mail was sent out, and brought in, on each helicopter trip.

Looking out across the valley one day, Don exclaimed, "There's the horse!" We all congregated outside to watch as Don walked across the valley, calling out to the horse. He offered it a handful of grass he'd plucked as he walked down the hill. According to Don, the farm guy, it was a mare with bay colouring. The horse, seemingly unafraid, allowed Don to walk right up to her. The field had more feed than our campsite, so we decided to leave her there. Whenever we saw her after that, we would go near enough to talk to her for a while. We were surprised at the healthy condition she was in after just coming through a winter. The next time the helicopter came in, we admitted to Rod we'd seen the horse, confirming what he'd claimed in his phone call to us last winter.

There was still a small patch of snow in a shaded area, in a gully across the valley. We'd all made one-dollar bets on what date it would disappear. As the days passed we got careless, watching it less and less frequently. One day Glen noticed that it was completely gone. No one was aware of the exact date it had disappeared, but everyone came to the conclusion that my bet was probably the closest. I was declared the winner, and the two men handed over their dollars. The three of us had quite compatible personalities. We each did our share of work and were always considerate towards one another. This made the close proximity required of camp living as pleasant as possible.

My loader driving lessons were increasing. Some days I was the only loader operator for the whole shift. My ability in operating it was now quite acceptable, and I managed a respectable load total at the end of the day. I still had to concentrate very hard, though, mentally counting each operating step of the big 930 loader as I went.

Don said to me one day, "Well, you aren't a full-fledged operator until you can do it without thinking, and can automatically push pedals and pull levers. Then you earn your pay."

"What pay?" I asked. "This is all voluntary. I was supposed to cook and be camp manager."

"Yeah, I know," said Don. "You really are doing okay."

When Don says someone is doing "okay" it really means they're doing very well. His words of praise were always well-earned.

The garden was still being inspected nightly; each leaf and flower was carefully nurtured. Water would flow as intended whenever we opened up the little dams or blocked off the little watercourses. The water had to go in slowly so that it wouldn't wash the delicate plants out of the soil. There were now enough plants growing that, when we looked towards our camp from the sluice-box, it appeared to be a green patch. I knew it would please Brian when he heard how well it was doing.

Ever since Forrest had left camp, Don had been working almost full-time on the bulldozer. It was a steady job of clearing trees and then removing the moss and top layers of dirt, gravel and permafrost. He also had to continually create ditches to take away the excess water run-off, because the permafrost melts once the moss covering is removed and it's exposed.

I don't remember how we got it, but to our dismay we received a notice saying that we'd done damage, and left debris, on our way from Pelly Ranch to Scroggie earlier. The environmental department was ordering us to repair this damage and collect the debris. The mess was created by someone else who had staked claims in the area that we were mining. However, we were the only ones who had done the proper thing and obtained a land-use permit before going over the trail.

Since we were the only name the department of environment had, we were held responsible. This was one time we really felt that honesty doesn't always pay.

Word had gotten out that we had a horse at Barker Creek. Across the Stewart River was a communal farm. Two men from the farm crossed the river and walked up to our camp. They had brought oats with them, and were interested in obtaining the horse. By this time the horse was quite friendly. She would come when Don called her, but always returned to the better feed across the valley afterwards.

We told the men the story we'd heard about how "Cooktent" – the name she went by – had been left to fend for herself. Apparently, she and one other horse had been taken into a mining camp on Thistle

Creek several years ago. The miners had abandoned the horses when they left. She was the only survivor, and had eventually wandered over the pass and down into Barker Valley. Always friendly, she spent her time begging for lumps of sugar at the cooktent. This was how she had earned her name.

The men said Cooktent would be useful at their farm and they could give her a good home. We told them we thought this was a great idea, and were sure that she would welcome the care she'd get. It was remarkable she'd survived as many winters as she had without it.

The men had lunch with us. During our conversation, we mentioned the notice we'd received. Before they left, we arranged to have them do the repair and clean up the garbage for a nominal fee. This was a big relief to us. It would have been difficult for us to have to shut down our mining and do it ourselves.

Next the two men explained how they planned on getting Cooktent home. They were going to walk back to Stewart River with her and then have her swim across the river behind their boat. A radio-phone call later let us know that Cooktent was safely on the farm. That is exactly where we felt she belonged.

Don and our garden; Yukon shower in the rear.

The sky blackened that afternoon and torrential rain began to fall. Soon after, loud thunderclaps seemed to shake the very earth itself, and streaks of lightning filled the sky. We had to call a halt to work for the day. In order for us not to waste the rest of the day, I decided to get extra cooking and baking done, and Glen and Don took inventory of the supplies. That same day, a radiophone message came from Forrest, asking if we really needed him. He had been offered a cat operator job and wondered if he should accept it.

"Forrest, take the job down there," Don said, and that's what Forrest did.

When mid-season arrived it was time for Glen to take his two-week holiday break, and return to the coast and the bright lights. The helicopter arrived with groceries and mail for us. Glen left with a grocery list and a roster of tasks to complete in Dawson on his way back.

CHAPTER 20

Lonely in the North

Don and I didn't figure we'd feel too deserted while Glen was gone, as we were anticipating the arrival of Cathy and our grandchildren in a week. We were excited about the prospect of seeing Mike and Dave, and having them play with the mining toys we'd purchased. I was also anticipating hearing their "oohs" and "ahs" in response to the special nursery-rhyme wallpaper in their bunkhouse. As the day wore on, we found it a bit strange to be just two people alone in the camp.

"Let's work longer before quitting for supper, and just have a hasty meal of anything that's easy and quick to prepare," suggested Don. That night it was pork and beans on toast, with canned fruit for dessert. We had scarcely any clean-up or dishes to do. We had our usual shower, and then relaxed with a book and the radio before tumbling into bed.

The week prior to Glen's holiday, we'd been getting less gold return each day. Don and I were wondering whether we should keep going where we were or try a new section of ground. We decided to persevere where we were, but to work a wider strip and do clean-ups more regularly. This would enable us to evaluate the ground. In other words, Don wanted to test the levels thoroughly, and try to determine what depth held the greatest amount of gold.

We were going through a difficult time. The amount of gold we were getting was diminishing. It was becoming obvious that the old river bed was not where we were working. It was going to take quite a bit more time to find it again. The bends and channels of any river change with the passing of time. The only thing we could do was to mine all across the bench and, where possible, go over the bank and down to the level that Barker Creek was presently running.

Don and I worked long hours each day, as it was mandatory to put as much gravel through the sluice as possible. Don was breaking bedrock, and some was already broken by nature. At Barker Creek, the bedrock lies quite flat, in slabs, from two to seven feet below the ground's surface. We had to put so much extra effort into digging and washing the pieces of bedrock, to get the gold that is supposed to lie on it. Being heavy, the gold works itself down through the less-compacted levels of ground until it gets to the bedrock. Landing here is like landing on a solid floor. The gold then lies here, unless the bedrock is broken, in which case it falls through the cracks.

These flat, squarish pieces are the ones that catch in the run of the sluice-box and cause a jam-up of rocks and water, requiring frantic efforts to clear the runway as fast as possible. The rounded, eroded, water-washed rocks in the gravel area above the bedrock go through the sluice-box quite easily. It is only the few that are larger in diameter than the rim of the box, that cause the problems. Sometimes we had to shut off the pump in order to get a rock jam cleared.

We stayed in this dead stretch for most of a week, and were becoming quite discouraged. We had all the equipment working, so the costs of operation were the same whether the day brought in good returns or not. At this point, the returns weren't cutting it. We were also missing Glen's infectious smile. The one bright spot in our thoughts was that Cathy, Mike and Dave were arriving the following day.

You can imagine our disappointment when a radio call came through early the next morning from Brian, telling us that the trio would not be coming. He told us that they'd talked it over, and because Linda and her children weren't able to come, they'd decided none of them would come this year. Brian may have been considering the extra expense. He knew that things were tough right now, and the gold this last month was below our expectations.

At any rate, this was the straw that broke the camel's back for me. I immediately burst into tears. It seemed that all the loneliness, hard work and problems that I'd suppressed for so long came to the fore. It was released all at once, in uncontrollable tears and sobs.

In spite of it all, Don and I went to work as usual, with me crying on and off most of the day. Soon my eyes were so red and swollen, I looked like I'd been on a week-long bender. Don decided to do a clean-up to see how much gold we'd accumulated from the last week's mining. Well, this was also a disaster. Just one more thing to bring on my flood of tears again. This day was certainly unproductive, and this extra letdown was beyond my acceptance level at the time. Conversation was nil, and self-pity was the envelope of the moment.

It was well past lunchtime, but neither of us had any appetite. Just then, a man stepped out of the bush. Glory be, we rarely got visitors, let alone pedestrian ones. Don started talking with him, and learned that he had his cat a short distance back in the bush. He was headed to do assessment work on claims upstream on Barker. The neighbourly thing to do was offer him lunch.

With tearstained, swollen eyes I made coffee and lunch for three. There was no way to keep my face hidden. Don and I weren't sure what the fellow must have been thinking. I made a feeble effort to explain my disappointment, but we have no idea whether the man believed my words. We wondered if he thought that either Don had beaten me, or we'd had a mighty row. At the time, I was still too upset to care what anyone thought. Don said very little the entire day. He knew how sad I felt, and he let me wallow in my sorrow.

Evening came, showers were taken, and we were off to bed – putting an end to the one and only day at camp that I'd given in to self-pity, tears and an overall inability to cope. Later Don claimed he didn't think I would have been safe operating a machine that day. That's why he'd suggested the clean-up. He was hoping it might be profitable and bring a ray of sunshine into that dismal day. He too had been feeling blue, but had worked very hard not to show it.

The following morning we were up as usual at 6 a.m. I told myself that I was no longer allowed the luxury of feeling sorry for myself. There was lots of work to be done, and I resolved to put 100-percent effort into doing my job. After a discussion of some length, Don and I decided we would have to volume-mine in order to produce sufficient yield to pay our bills. We made a pact to work longer hours with no self-pity, despite it being lonely out there, miles from anyone. If you let your mind run away, the thoughts could be rather terrifying. This very isolation caused us to take every precaution against accidents happening. At all times, we were extremely safety conscious.

The area we were digging and sluicing was becoming very noticeable. Our twelve-hour, sometimes longer, days were showing in the volume sluiced. When Glen arrived back in three days, he would see a big difference. We were hoping by that time we'd be back in good-paying gravel. We were working an area of about 150 by 100 feet,

Gwen learning to drive the 930 loader.

digging approximately six feet deep. When we began this section we had been close to the sluice-box. Now we were 200 to 300 feet from it. This meant a longer travel time for each bucketful. Consequently, our "total loads" count was not as high at the end of the day.

We planned on working in this manner for a few more days. Then we'd do another clean-up, to see if the overall yield of gold had improved, or if we were continuing to work in a non-productive stretch of ground. When we did these clean-ups, we immediately gathered up the coarser nuggets. The remainder went onto the Deister table.

In the end, we realized that it had probably been a good thing that Cathy and the children hadn't come. We'd been having only dull, cloudy, chilly days with many sprinkles of rain throughout the week. It would have been difficult to keep Mike and Dave happily occupied in that weather.

Don now had to curtail the sluicing while he did more stripping. He had to channel the mud to keep it from entering the creek. The heavy rains would have flooded our garden too, but we deepened the little trenches between the rows, and opened up the ends in order to lead the excess water over the bank. The garden was growing well and was such a pleasant site, that we put a lot of effort into protecting the growing plants.

About this time we had another visitor. This one came by air – Mr. Rothwell, from the Yukon Water Board. He wrote out a favourable report. He could see that we were trying to follow the guidelines, and that we were doing our work in an environmentally agreeable fashion.

The next day the creek was extremely swollen and it had gathered a lot of debris. The fast-moving water put our pump in danger. Don and I clad ourselves in rain gear and began pulling out all the branches that were functioning like a dam in the creek; they had accumulated with the flooding of it. Don was going to have to take the cat down close to the creek again. It would be a repeat performance from once before. He put a winch line around a log, tied the line around the platform on which the pump sat, and prayed that the water would soon subside. It was very chilly. I had a pair of Don's long johns on, and I put a towel around my shoulders to keep the rain from running down my neck and back.

Rod flew in with the chopper that day to bring us our long-awaited mail. A six-week postal strike had finally ended. We had letters from all of the family. My sister Pat, an employee at Lee's Jade and Opals, and Brian sent a detailed report on the business. Pat had just celebrated her fiftieth birthday. Enclosed with the report was a snap-shot of Pat and her cake. What was she doing in the photo? Well, her cake, like Colonel Sanders' chicken, must have been finger-lickin' good, because she was licking the icing off her fingers.

Brian's main message was, "Shop is chugging along nicely; all bills are paid. It's too bad things have been so tough for you both, but I think you are being too hard on yourselves. It would seem we have to put more gravel through the sluice-box, and of course that will mean we buy more equipment, and more workers. Do you think we should consider taking in a partner?"

It's a sentimental time when we read letters from home. My mom mentioned how disappointed we must have been that Cathy, Mike and Dave did not come to the Yukon. Likely that's why she wrote an extra long and newsy letter.

Besides news through letters, we also received a phone call from Glen that day. He told us that all was fine in Langley, including the weather. It was good to hear from him. We told him how the creek was in flood stage, and we'd be spending the day doing camp chores.

We split wood that day, and then I baked bread and cookies to sweeten our disposition. After this, we checked on the water level and the safety of the pump. All seemed okay, so we resumed hauling grav-el and putting it through the sluice-box for the next four hours. Then everything came to a sudden halt. Don noticed a breakthrough in a section of the wall of one of the settling ponds. Immediately he left the sluicing to deal with it. The ground was too soft to get the cat near, therefore we had to haul extra dirt by wheelbarrows. Then we used bucketfuls of dirt to reinforce the edge. It was extremely hard work.

Don's stomach was upset. No doubt it was from the extra work and stress. The rain finally stopped so we decided to go for a walk to get our minds away from work. It was a pleasant change. The air was perfumed with the many wild flowers that were now in bloom, and we relaxed a little.

On our return to camp we had a hot chocolate drink, and began planning our work for the following day. Don suggested that we put the sluice-box on a steeper angle so that the water and gravel would go through quicker. This would enable us to work through this poor stretch of ground in less time, and hopefully be on to something better soon. The wet weather we were experiencing made a lot of mud. This caused travel with the loader to become very slippery. This was yet another worry for us to contend with.

That night the weather increased in severity. Rain pelted down, thunder roared and lightning filled the sky. Suddenly, a high wind came up and a gust blew the five-gallon water bucket from the top of the shower, sending it rolling down the hill toward the creek. Next the wind lifted a sheet of plywood and carried it sailing across the camp to land 100 feet away. The shower was unusable that evening, so out came the galvanized washtub. We had our bath in the cosiness of our cabin, which was heated with the very reliable airtight heater. Even though it was midsummer, after a few wet days there was a definite chill to the air. The quick heat from the airtight heater radiated welcome warmth before bedtime.

The next day Don did the repairs necessitated by the previous night's wind damage, and soon we were back to the daily routine. We knew that our results depended on extending our work hours and accelerating our production. In order to keep a commitment made to ourselves as well as to others, we had to use extra will power and determination to make this a successful year.

Gold mining got inordinately tough this summer. When things seemed the darkest and most difficult, we gave ourselves a pep talk. We'd say things like, "We are very fortunate. We have our health, as do our children, grandchildren and the rest of our family." We only had to think back to last November, when our close friends lost their twenty-six-year-old son to leukemia, and my sister's best friends lost their twenty-two-year-old son in a house fire, to recognize how blessed we were. Once again we tried to look for the silver lining hidden in the cloud of the moment. . . .

It was July 1981. The reception on our short-wave radio was excellent as we tuned in to the pomp and pageantry of Prince Charles and Princess Diana's wedding. It sounded so beautiful and luxurious. I hung on every word of descriptive splendour. I couldn't help making comparisons to our station in life. Here we were, two people out in the immense north, miles from anyone. We were clad in work pants that had recently been equipped with ventilation due to holes, and workboots with broken, knotted laces.

Our construction caterpillar and loader were our royal carriages. Gourmet food? Well, we had our basic healthy lot. The glitter of their finished gems and jewellery was our search for gold.

I conjured up a mental picture of their ceremony – its beauty, solemnity, happiness and perhaps a little sadness. In dream-like fashion I was carried through the wedding and the reception following. Later I would read the books and look at the photographs that covered the event. At this moment, though, I just took an imaginary visit to the enchanted-fairyland atmosphere. Don and I created the mental image we wanted it to be. We certainly couldn't disregard what many others might see as our very own fairy-tale marriage. We were always empathetic and considerate towards one another. We also had a special closeness that had developed in our thirty-three years together. We were very lucky to have each other and the unique love we shared. On this night, though, we celebrated the royal wedding, and went to bed with something new to think and dream about.

CHAPTER 21

Mud as Dangerous as Quicksand

We were delighted to hear the sound of the helicopter as it descended. Glen had returned. Don and I assisted the pilot and Glen with unloading groceries and the other supplies that we'd requested Glen bring. Then I made coffee and a snack and we spent the next hour eating and chatting. Glen filled us in on all the news, including that from Dawson City. He said it was very busy – every hotel and motel was filled to capacity. Ursula had pitched a tent for him on her grounds. This was where Glen had spent the night, but the cost had still equalled that of a room.

The equipment and Barker Creek camp.

There was Jergens hand lotion among the supplies Glen had brought in. He'd purchased it for me – how sweet! I hadn't asked for it, but before he'd left camp he'd noticed my hands were getting rough and callused. When I thanked him, he said, "Every lady likes Jergens lotion."

Glen had also brought us more letters from home. To this day we still have all of the letters we received. Many of the ones that we wrote on the roll of turquoise-green paper and sent out from camp to our family have also been kept. These letters, and the diaries Don and I kept, are the substance for the story I'm now relating. Of course, like us, the paper has gathered crinkles and wrinkles over the years, but it survived with the messages intact.

Glen was surprised at the amount of gravel we'd put through the sluice-box. He and Don resumed the outside work while I put away the groceries. Glen and Don took up their routines again. However, as the days passed Don and I began noticing his quietness, and the sad, faraway look that always seemed to be in his eyes. We wondered if it might be the fact that he'd so recently gotten married. He'd had to leave his bride to commence the mining season, and his recent trip home may have made him wish he hadn't come to the Yukon.

Glen's mother and I had worked together and been neighbours all our pre-marriage years. This made Glen far closer to us than had he been an ordinary employee. Finally Don inquired, "What's troubling you, Glen?"

"I'm missing the Fraser Valley, and my sister isn't very well," Glen replied.

In spite of wanting to stay in the Fraser Valley, Glen's sense of loyalty had brought him back to the Yukon. Glen was a good worker, a loyal friend and a pleasant person by nature. We didn't like to see him upset. Consequently, Don said, "Glen, if your heart is in the Fraser Valley, and you want to go, that's okay. But it has to be your decision. All we ask is that you go out on a helicopter that is bringing goods to camp, so we don't have the cost of the extra trip."

Glen said he'd think about it. He made several radiophone calls home, and a few days later said to us, "I guess I'll go."

Meanwhile we did another clean-up. The gold continued to be

fine and not in sufficient quantity. Since the results hadn't improved sufficiently to stay in that area, Don decided to move the sluice-box and work a different section. We had to decide where the best place on the property would be. After some thought, we figured we should go back to the spot we'd started on in the spring, but work in the opposite direction.

We needed to be about the same distance from the creek as the spot that we'd just been working on. We'd have to move the pump, but we didn't want to have to go through the trouble of lengthening the water hose, or the extra work that it would require if we weren't able to use the same settling ponds. Time was of the essence, and fall would come all too quickly.

There was almost daily conversation with Brian, Linda and the business. They all continued to write letters to us as well. In these they each frankly stated the facts, and suggested alternatives. Brian's letters were always encouraging. He kept saying, "Don't be so hard on yourselves; you are both working too hard."

I assured him that my muscles were building up – not that I particularly wanted big muscles – and that it just went with the job. I told him that soon I'd be able to tear telephone directories in half – something I'd seen a body builder do.

We told Brian that Glen had decided to leave. We were going to send some gold out with him. He'd get it recorded at the Dawson mining office before boarding the plane for home. I also informed Brian that I'd be writing a longer letter, which Glen would deliver to him.

The garden was doing well. This was one of our constant pleasures, because of the aesthetic value as well as the salad makings it was providing. We were getting fresh lettuce, radishes and green onions every day. The potato plants were healthy looking. They were about a foot high and there was eight inches of carrot tops showing. The tomato plants had small green tomatoes too. On bright sunny days we could almost see the plants growing.

The evenings got very cool, so we began banking up the cookhouse heater before retiring. On rising in the morning, red coals could still be seen, the kettle of water that we'd put on the heater the previous evening was hot, and coffee could quickly be made by the camp-style, open-pot method.

Rivers of Gold   163

The trees had been cleared from behind the cabins. Don had taken them down and removed the topsoil. This was the spot where we'd decided to take the next gravel from. Not having previously planned to do this section, he wasn't finished the stripping that would enable the permafrost to melt. This usually occurs first so that the gravel is ready to put in the sluice-box. Working with frozen gravel necessitated breaking it up with the aid of the ripper on the bulldozer before it could be picked up with the loader, transported and put through the sluice-box.

Don was really pushing to get gravel exposed and moved into a pile close enough to the present road. He did this so that he wouldn't have to go over the recently removed moss covering from the permafrost ground. He threw caution to the wind a little, and then had almost more than he could handle of melting permafrost that was making the mud slide. He frantically deepened his ditches. Cutting through the frozen ground was slow work.

One evening Don thought the mud had beaten him. It was sliding at a rapid rate, right in line with our camp. At the last moment, some guardian angel must have decided the mud had travelled far enough. It abruptly stopped, just a few feet from one of the cabins. Don sighed with relief, but wasn't fully over his concern.

"I'm going to get up every two hours tonight and do a check on the mud," he said. "The cooler night air will help to slow down the sliding, but we can't take any unnecessary chances." Consequently we set the alarm, and dutifully got up for this inspection.

The rain had finally stopped, and patches of blue sky were showing through the cloudy sky. We could even see the sun! After a couple of sunny days, the wet areas were beginning to dry up. The newly exposed areas of permafrost were beginning to get muddy, and the water was running from them. Don had to be careful to avoid getting the machine stuck. Glen had begun taking turns on the D6 cat, so he too could understood Don's precautions.

Don had pulled the log storage building ahead 25 feet, bringing it neatly in line with the other buildings. We could now mine the ground it had previously sat on. Of course, before moving this building, we had to empty all of its contents, and then replace them once it was in its new place.

This log storage building was the one that the men had constructed without peeling the logs first. Termites live just under the bark of the trees so if the logs aren't peeled, the termites eat the logs. Now, a multitude of little mounds of sawdust had developed around the perimeter of the building. We could actually hear the little creatures chewing away inside the logs. It sounded like a bunch of grasshoppers, and the noise was continuous. Had the logs been peeled, Glen, Don and I would not have had to listen to their "crunch, crunch, munch" while they continuously made lunch out of our log building!

Surprisingly, there'd been very few mosquitoes this year. Glen doesn't like bugs, so he freely commented on the number of flies. The flies appeared with the sunny days, but fortunately they weren't the biting kind. With the sun, buds had also appeared. Some were almost open on the California poppies and nasturtiums. One more bright day, and they'd pop into bloom.

While Don and Glen relocated the sluice-box, drove the cat and moved the building, I took this time to bake and to make meals that had a longer preparation time. When Glen did the grocery shopping in Dawson, the store was out of salad dressing, so I had to make up my own recipe. It was actually quite good, although it definitely wouldn't have put Miracle Whip in danger of being replaced.

For the first time we had three graylings that Don had caught in the creek. They were a real tasty treat, but because they were very bony, they required skilful fork work to separate the fish from the bones to make them edible. Don said, "We should treat ourselves again to a catch of fresh fish." However, we never got around to it.

Glen had begun doing the final setting up of the sluice-box in its new location. This required welding. He was making every effort to have it ready to begin putting the gravel through the following day. He and Don were some distance apart, each in opposite directions from the cookhouse. It was nearing afternoon coffee time, so I went to the cookhouse, poured the mugs of coffee and buttered muffins. I took Glen his first, since he was nearer at hand.

I decided I'd take my coffee and muffin with me, along with Don's, so we could enjoy the break together. I put it all on a ten-inch round tray and set off. The new area Don was working was further than usual from camp. Separating this area from the camp was an area of recently uncovered permafrost ground. It was now beginning to crust over, harden, and accrue cracks in the surface. I looked down at the mud and cracks, and thought, "It looks fairly dry; I think it will hold my weight, and I can take a short cut to where Don is working."

After gingerly putting my foot on it, and thinking it felt quite firm, I put my other foot on. Yes, it seemed sufficiently substantial. My first few steps went fine, so step by step I proceeded. After going approximately 150 feet, it began to get softer. Walking was becoming difficult, but I still felt I'd be okay if this was as bad as it was going to get. I took a few more steps and started to sink. The mud was now beginning to cover my canvas runners. Instead of realizing the difficult situation I was getting into, my only thoughts were, "Damn, my clean shoes are getting all dirty. Now I'll have to wash them."

One or two more steps and the bells began to ring loud and clear! I couldn't pick either foot up. I was getting sucked into a sea of mud. I began to panic, but I knew that yelling wouldn't do any good. Both Don and Glen had big machines going and wouldn't have heard me. Glen couldn't see the area I was in from where he was, and Don had his back to me. With great effort, I pulled one foot out, leaving the shoe behind. Then I did the same thing with the other foot. Thank goodness the canvas shoes were loose enough to slide easily from my feet. They quickly got swallowed up in the mud. I still had my socks on.

Visions came to me of a movie I'd once seen in which a man sank out of sight in quicksand. He slowly got swallowed up, until only his shoulders and head showed above the surface. Eventually, there was only a bubble to show where the man had once been. "Is this to be my fate?" I wondered.

By now my socks had been sucked up too. Then I remembered the old adage: If you find yourself on breaking ice, or in quicksand, lie on your stomach and creep. I got down on all fours and began inching along. I was gaining ground, getting back to firmer mud. It was at this moment that Don happened to glance my way. He did a marathon race to the road to come and rescue me. I looked up to see Don shoving a stick at me. This helped with the final few feet to firm ground.

166

It was a traumatic experience. I was shaken up enough that I didn't do anything for the rest of the day. I'm not sure if it was Don or myself who was more upset, thinking about what could have been. I guess my number just wasn't meant to be up yet. Only a pair of runners and socks were claimed by the Barker mud that day. The tray and mugs were rescued a few days later – they weren't heavy enough to be swallowed up in the liquid mud. Since that experience, I have a lot more respect for soft ground and water.

CHAPTER 22

Just the Two of Us

Rod Watt, the helicopter pilot, called and told us that Dave Jennings at the mining office was interested in seeing a few of the mining operations on the creeks. Rod had told him about ours because it was a small, neat operation. Others had been chosen because they were large ones.

"Would it be okay if I brought him in to see yours?" Rod asked. We told him it would be fine – in fact, we'd welcome the visit. Rod told us to expect him in a few days. Knowing that the chopper was coming in, we made arrangements for Glen to leave camp at the same time.

Don was beginning to look like a wild man. He'd let his hair grow, and hadn't shaved since he'd come into camp this season. This was unusual for Don. He had always worn his hair in a crew cut that was continually in and out of style, depending on the times. Now he'd decided maybe his hair should be trimmed a little. One evening I obliged. I reminded myself of the adage, "The difference between a good or poor haircut is about two weeks." I cut a little. It didn't look straight, so I cut a little more. Then I had to re-cut the other side to match. I realized by the end of the haircut that barbering was more than just holding the scissors and comb. I didn't offer to cut the back; I just did a little trimming around the ears. Don's mirrored reflection told me that he wasn't at all impressed with my skills.

We tried the sluice-box at a slightly higher elevation. Steepening it meant that more gravel could go through at a quicker rate. Hopefully, this would end the dead stretch we were in, and we could get back to the good-paying gravel. The season was passing rapidly, and time was precious.

One of the days started out cloudy. The sun showed up for a while, but by 4 p.m. heavy rain began falling. We couldn't put the work off, even in this weather. In fact, Don and Glen had an extra job to do that evening. They had to remove the old sidearms from the cat, and then put on the new ones that had come in the helicopter with Glen on his return to camp.

The rain continued through the night, and on into the next morning. After putting only five loads through the sluice-box, we had to stop. The water leaving the sluice-box started to break through a sidewall and run in the wrong direction. Don took the D6 cat and with the ripper, slashed through the frozen ground as hastily as possible, to make another run-off ditch. A large quantity of rocks from the previous sluicing had slid to the bottom of the hill. Don was able to use this material to make the ditch sidewalls and keep the water flowing where we could control it. This took five hours. Then it was back to sluicing.

Rain continued to pour right into the next day. The recently stripped ground was not drying as it should because of this, so whether we liked it or not, work got delayed. Everything was too muddy, and this posed the possibility of Don getting the cat stuck. This would cause work to cease altogether. Mining and farming have a lot in common. Owners and employees have to constantly worry about either too much or too little rain.

It's doubtful that anyone who has not been involved in mining can imagine the hours put into building and maintaining the roads, ponds and ditches. People often read about the hardships that the old prospectors and miners endured, but it isn't much different in this day and age. Mining is hard work. Time has to be spent on equipment maintenance. Machinery is costly, and water supply and weather are major factors.

I had Glen take a picture of me while I was wearing men's large-size rain gear with my pants and sleeves rolled up. I didn't have any rain gear of my own, therefore I had two options. I could get soaked, or put on the men's. I chose the latter.

Another day went by, and finally the skies began to clear up. We were able to work with no problems on this day. Late that afternoon Rod brought Dave Jennings, the mining inspector, over in the helicopter. We were pleased to have them join us for supper. Dave was surprised to see our well-painted and decorated camp. He was also impressed with our little garden.

It turned out that Glen was going to have to remain in camp for a few more days. Rod had to pick up two miners who urgently needed to get to Dawson that night. Rod knew that there was no urgency for Glen to depart.

We were supposed to have had eight barrels of fuel flown in with the big 204 helicopter, but forest fires in the Northwest Territories had taken the machine from service here. Instead, we would have to use an Alouette 3 helicopter, which could only bring us four barrels at a time. This was going to be more expensive, but we needed fuel so we had no alternative.

I wrote Brian to keep him abreast of our problems with the mine operation. On rereading the letter years later, two things stood out. The first thing was, "We still have faith in the property, but we are too few people. We should have the equipment running double shift, and then we'd soon swallow up the area and get through the dead stretches much quicker." The second was, "Brian, keep this letter. Maybe some day we can all reread it and laugh about it." Years later we could.

Meanwhile I had become a good loader operator. I proved my skills by taking loads of the topsoil, gravel and permafrost to the edge and dumping it down the 130-foot embankment. I admit I was a little nervous about having to get the wheels close enough to the edge to ensure that the material I was dumping would make it over. While I was doing this, Don was preparing new ground, stripping and piling the material I was hauling away. He was confident that I was able to do the job, and not go over the bank with the loader. I had been as jumpy as a cat on a hot tin roof during the first four loads, and at that point, if it hadn't been so essential, I would have refused to do it.

Fine collection of gold nuggets.

Don at Barker Creek with the gold spinner.

However, since it was, I used full concentration and care, and managed to cautiously begin and successfully complete the job of dumping material over the edge.

We were all anxious to begin putting gravel through the sluice-box once again. We were hoping to see lots of yellow in the riffles here. After moving to a new location, it is very important that more detailed testing be done, by panning. Don began in the conventional miner position – kneeling at the creek. This is really hard on the back. After briefly working this way, Don said, "To heck with that back-breaking job. I'll get a barrel, fill it with water, and pan in the barrel in a standing position." There were lots of 45-gallon fuel barrels around, so a barrel was soon placed in a convenient place. We burned it out first, to eliminate any grease, and then filled it with the garden hose. The job was then completed in this manner.

Every once in a while, I'd allow myself a little time for sorrow. I still got choked up with tears whenever I thought about the guest-house not getting used this year. Every time I walked by it, small pangs pulled at my heartstrings. I would think back to the time I had decorated it, getting it ready for the grandchildren's visit.

I felt sorry for myself, because I was out here in this isolated area, working so hard. It seemed that the longer and harder the work day, the deeper the hole of debt we were digging. I felt sorry for Don, who had worked so hard, and was seeing his efforts, and dreams of gold, crumbling around him, replaced only with worry. I felt sorry for Glen, who seemed so unhappy, and for Brian, who was doing his best at the shop and continually giving us support due to his concern for our plight. When these moods overcame me, all I could do was cross my fingers, and hope that with the move to new gravel, our circumstances would change.

Everything was ready for the start of the sluicing operation in the new area. We put sixty loads through as a trial run. It looked hopeful. We were working in cramped quarters, as only the essential dirt was being moved. We wanted to spend as little time as possible building a flat turnaround area to enable us to begin putting gravel through the sluice-box and to find out if we were hitting pay dirt. Part of the ground that I was driving the loader on was still frozen, and very uneven. I often felt like I was going to tip, but so far the wheels had remained in contact with the ground. I had to raise the bucket higher to dump the loads here, because of the steep incline of the dumping box.

Glen worked the sluice-box, raking the rocks through. Don, who was on the cat, was loosening and piling the gravel that I was hauling to the sluice-box. This was how we would work for the next little while.

Glen was obviously having a difficult time with his decision to leave. The day before he'd told us that he was going to stay, but today he reverted back to his former plan. He said he'd leave when the next helicopter came in. Don and I didn't have that privilege. We had to stay, put in the full season, and then make an evaluation at the close of it.

Everyone was feeling in the dumps, so I did the one thing I could to bring a little cheer into our lives – I tried to make the meals as attractive and tasty as I could. We had spinach from the garden. It was lovely and tender, but I'd had to take the whole row for a mere three servings. The Swiss chard was ready now, so for the next dinner I'd decided to make that our green vegetable.

There were a few sparrows and swallows that regularly came around for crumbs and other offerings that were placed outside the cookhouse door. They seemed to know just when it was mealtime. I think they must have kept their eye on anyone that was heading towards the cookhouse. Gradually the number of birds that were coming for handouts increased. One sparrow flew right into the cookhouse. I wondered if that was a good omen. I'd have to wait and see.

After dinner we treated ourselves to a "sit down" outdoors. A hill hid the sun from us from just after 6 p.m. until 9 p.m. Then it reappeared until just after 10 p.m. This hour in-between was the nicest one of the day. There was seldom any wind, so it was the hour we usually chose to have our showers and read, before calling it a day.

We were now starting to put gravel through the box from the new area. Colours were appearing in the riffles. It looked like the move was an improvement. We decided to put the bedrock through the sluice-box if the pieces were a manageable size. If the bedrock has been cracked by nature, it can have trapped gold in it that can be washed out. Even though the surface is flat, bedrock pieces have extremely rough edges and can easily cause jams in the sluice-box. Wrestling with chunks of bedrock is tough work. We all needed an Absorbine Jr rubdown after this!

The helicopter arrived just as we were all turning in for the night. Rod had brought in the mining tags we'd requested – they got fastened to stakes to identify our claims. He was going straight back to Dawson, so he said he could take Glen out with him on this trip. This way, we'd only have to pay for a split trip.

Glen was ready within minutes. He had been packed and ready to go for several days. We sure had lumps in our throats when Glen left. Don and I would now be on our own. It was going to be a busy and somewhat lonely time for us. The one consolation – if there was one – was that we would only have to consider each other. We could now work any length of day we wanted, and eat our meals accordingly.

CHAPTER 23

The H-U-G-E Nugget

The first morning without Glen, Don decided to do extra ditching. He suggested that I bake and cook – he wanted some extra meals made and frozen for later use, since he knew we were going to have to spend the majority of our time mining. These precooked meals were a boon in the days to follow.

As usual, we were in constant communication with both our family and the shop. Glen took my letter to give to Brian. In it I gave Brian all the details of our recent mining. I knew Glen would also assure Brian that all was well here at the camp.

Don and I commenced the sluicing and bedrock-lifting tango. The two of us were continually struggling with the pieces that were too large to go through the sluice-box. Often, after a day of lifting the pieces, we would tally up the number of bruises each of us had amassed. Of course it was Don who had to wrestle with the really huge pieces, always trying to avoid taking the time to use the loader to chain them and hoist them out of the dumping box. It made my heart ache to see him working so hard.

If we were lucky, we'd spot the large pieces as the loader bucket was getting filled. In those cases we'd try to remove them immediately and push them onto the waste pile. After doing this, we often wondered if there wasn't gold clinging to the piece and that we should have washed it off.

Talking to Brian on the radiophone, we found out that Glen had done the necessary gold recording and paid the royalty in Dawson City. He had also given out the letters we had written, and had brought Brian up to date on all of our other news. Glen told Brian that his parents were working very hard.

A few days later, we had a terrific thunderstorm. Crashing thunder drummed the skies and lightning as bright as a welder's flash lit the entire valley. The thunder and lightning came almost instantaneously one upon the other. It was the worst storm we'd been in since leaving Manitoba, a place known for its severe thunderstorms. Neither of us slept much that night. Don was worried we'd have another mudslide because of all the recently exposed dirt.

It continued to rain the next morning, so Don decided to push the fresh dirt and overburden into piles. I had to follow with the loader; load by load I took it and dumped it in a safe place to avoid any chance of an uncontrollable mudslide. Most of the day was spent doing this, but at least it meant we could sleep peacefully that night.

Since Glen had left, we'd been working until at least 7 p.m. before breaking for supper. On the nights that Don did the equipment maintenance, I did the laundry, baking and cooking. During this time of nonstop work, we heard on the radio that Dawson was going to be celebrating Discovery Days on the coming weekend. Conversations between the camps confirmed that some of the miners would be going to Dawson for this event. Not anyone from Barker Creek! The usual daily routine was to preside here.

Our next radiophone call came from Herman. He told us he'd either be coming over to Barker camp in a helicopter, or would send one to bring us to Scroggie so we could meet with him. Don and I had visions of the cheque that was due to us, so we agreed to meet him at

Scroggie. The meeting took place on August 5th. Our happiness was soon shattered when he announced that he did not have the money. However, he said he would have it in a few days. He explained that he was leaving camp in order to arrange the payment. Herman claimed he would send it to our Langley address after phoning Brian. We received neither the phone call nor the payment.

Rod had a friend who wanted to come to stay with us for a few days. We wondered if Rod was sending a visitor to Barker because he was concerned about us. We assured Rod that his friend was welcome. Don asked if he could bring along spray paint, tags and other things we were in need of. Rod and Steve showed up by helicopter at Barker with all the requested items. As usual, we had our mail brought in at the same time.

Steve was interested in watching how gold mining was done. He asked if he could do a little panning.

"Try it at the end of the sluice-box," Don said. Darned if he didn't find a nice-sized nugget which we had lost in our clean-up. We told him that he'd found it, so it was his. We've often wondered if he still has it. It was large enough to use as a pendant.

For three consecutive nights there had been a frost. The first one came on August 17th. The hillside trees were all turning golden. Some leaves had already fallen, and skeletal branches were showing in places. This was the first reminder that autumn would soon be upon us, and our mining season was almost up. There was a thin film of ice in the sluice-box each morning, and we couldn't start sluicing until it melted.

The days were bright and sunny, though – the nicest we'd had all season. We were able to use our outdoor shower, and there was ample daylight for our pre-bedtime reading. We had to pick the lettuce, put six heads in our cooler, and eat the carrots and potatoes. We should have been eating them sooner, but we didn't want to pull our garden apart, it was looking so beautiful. The potatoes were large – up to four inches long – and scab-free. Some of the flowers had frozen, and Don noticed the first of the sandhill cranes flying south.

The move to new ground was proving to be a good idea. We were getting good-sized nuggets, some an ounce or more. We were elated. We still had a chance of making a profit, although this got slimmer daily. We were sluicing as many hours as possible every day, because we only had two weeks left. We had made arrangements to be taken to Dawson the weekend following Labour Day.

One day was spoiled because a pin broke on the D6 cat. We had to have Finning send another. A rush helicopter was called for and George, the pilot, came with the pin. Steve, who'd been with us several days, went out with the helicopter. Having Steve around had been good for Don and me. He'd helped us do a clean-up, and had aided in putting tags on claims.

After Steve left, we went back to the longer working day. We started with other chores each morning, because of the ice in the sluice-box. We walked to Dixie Creek, put tags on those claims, and then we measured each area of work we'd done on Barker Creek. This was required by the government so that we could file our assessment work for the year.

As we walked in the light rain to Dixie, we talked about all that had transpired since we'd first tramped this trail with our laden John Deere. Just as we crossed the creek, a rainbow appeared. It was almost like a step back in time. The rainbow emerged only briefly and then disappeared. Perhaps it was saying farewell to us.

Since we were alone once again, Don and I decided to have a picnic. We took our lunch over to Iron Creek. We also did some test holes on the claims there. We decided to do sufficient stripping, beginning the following morning, for the required assessment work for the year.

The cooler weather brought with it the return of the beautiful northern lights, with their fantastic array of colours. Each time we saw them, we stood in awe, admiring their shimmering beauty as they danced across the sky. Mornings were chilly, however, and the ice in the sluice-box wasn't melting until after 11 a.m. Even so, we were successful in our nightly search for nuggets in the riffles.

We had a glorious surprise on August 24th. We had sluiced from noon until nearly 8 p.m. We stopped for supper, and then went out to dig in the riffles to collect the larger nuggets. Most of the gold, especially the heavy nuggets, are found in the first few riffles at the top end of the box. Daily, after the sluicing water had been turned off, we picked out these nuggets. At one time, Don had used his favourite spoon for this. Its handle was bent at just the right angle for digging in the riffles. He'd lost it in our previous clean-up, so this time he had to use an ordinary spoon, like myself.

I accepted my usual spot, several feet down the box. This was where the medium to small nuggets generally settled. It was like an unwritten law, that I wasn't to get in those top riffles – the pecking order had long ago been established. On bent knees, we were at our stations at the sluice-box, digging in among the riffles. The sun was shining on the remnants of moisture. It was making the metal glisten, so when I noticed this golden "ball", I wasn't really sure what I was seeing. It was about two-thirds the size of a golf ball. I stood transfixed as it glistened and winked.

"Is that a nugget?" I thought quickly. "Can't be – wouldn't happen in my riffles – look at the size." I figured it must be one of the yellow-gold coloured rocks that have no value. I knew that as soon as I picked it up, I would definitely know if it was gold or not by the weight. I wanted so badly to believe it was gold that I just savoured the next few seconds, enjoying the spell of the moment. With high hopes, I reached for it. Wow! The weight was there. It had to be gold!

At the same time, Don was industriously going through his section of the riffles. I could barely close the palm of my hand over the nugget. As calmly and nonchalantly as I could manage, I turned to Don and said, "Don, hold out your hand. I've found something you want."

"Oh, you've found my spoon," Don responded, without looking up.

"No," I said, "better than that – look!"

Don raised his eyes. Surprise and awe quickly registered on his face. "Wow! Wow! How much do you think it weighs? Do you think it will be seven and a half ounces – or better?" he rambled.

We had heard that a seven-and-a-half-ounce nugget had been found on the property next to ours some years ago. It was the largest for the area.

We ran into the cookhouse, where the scales were located. Before we'd even weighed our nugget, Don said, "We're toasting it with Scotch." He poured us each a drink, and then proceeded to get out the little forty-pennyweight (two-ounce) scale. He tried to devise a balance to weigh the nugget. It took quite a lot of improvising, but he said, "I'm sure it's a full seven and a half ounces."

Did that ever make our day – especially with the addition of the other nuggets that were over an ounce. We were back in pay gravel!

The large nugget (pictured on the cover) was not a good-looking nugget. It was too round and smooth. We were working in the broken bedrock area, and surmised that the gold had been trapped with water in a cavity in the broken rock. It had probably tumbled around, wearing the rough edges off the nugget and leaving a smooth ball shape. This was probably also the reason that this nugget had travelled so far down the sluice-box. Whatever the case, it was a lovely sight and size. We couldn't wipe the smiles off our faces that night.

In the days that followed, the gold yield continued to be good. By this time there were no doubts that we'd be able to pay all of the bills for the season. We'd even end up with leftover gold to sell or keep, as we chose.

We continued to haul mud in the evening. Don used the cat to get the three to five feet of overburden away from the gravel that we wanted to put through the sluice-box. He couldn't push it over a bank, or it would get the creek muddy, and there was nowhere close by to dump it. That's when the loader was brought in. With it, I scooped up the mud and hauled it to an area where it wouldn't cause a problem. The rubber tires on the loader made travelling much faster than the tracks on the cat would have. We had forty barrels of fuel left, but didn't figure we'd end up using it all.

Working outside all day in the sun had endowed us with fantastic tans. Don usually burns from the sun, but this time he was quite brown. We looked as if we'd just returned from a six-week vacation in Mexico. I can assure you there was one difference, though – at Barker Creek there were no siestas!

With only the two of us working, the focus was on sluicing. Don and I decided to take turns driving the loader and dumping gravel in the sluice-box. While one of us was doing this job, the other raked the rocks through the sluice-box run. Changing jobs seemed to break the monotony and make the day go faster. Don kept the cat nearby, so he could continue to clear the rocks away when they piled up at the end of the box run.

Except for the occasional showers, we had two weeks of very

pleasant weather. Only a few flowers remaine,
continued to be frost at night. Our nights and .
cool. We spent one evening cutting firewood fron.
en the past spring. We also dismantled the old tent fr.
for firewood. This was so that we could continue to hav.
morning and evening.

We had come to our final sluicing day. The gravel we hac   .red
and piled for sluicing was finished, and we decided that it wasn't worth
trying to get any more. The ice on the sluice-box wasn't melting until
noon, and of course, we couldn't sluice until it was gone. We had to
count our blessings this year, though. The year before the weather had
been much worse – the first snowfall had come on September 2nd. This
year, except for the occasional time when we had to haul in the old galvanized laundry tub for a bath, we were still able to use our outside
shower.

I scanned the cupboard each morning and decided what could
be used up, since we didn't want to bring in another grocery order
before leaving. There was lots of walnuts and brown sugar left, so I
made a batch of fudge. There was very little flour left, so I had to
stretch it with either bran, oats or cornmeal.

On September 12th we prepared everything in the camp for storage. We'd used the Deister table to separate our gold, and gathered
up some of the heavy black sand in a drum. Our plan was to send it
out to a refinery next year to have the fine gold left in it processed.
We rolled up the hoses and stored them. They would no longer be of
any use to the garden, as the hard frost the night before had finished
it. It was now a sad-looking sight.

We oiled and greased the machinery and put antifreeze in the
radiators. Next we serviced all the equipment. Each piece was either
placed in the storage shed or carefully covered with tarps. Our camp
was getting tucked in for a long winter nap.

Chores were coming to an end, and we were going to be leaving
any day now. One of our last jobs was to make a complete inventory
list. We knew if we didn't make one, we'd never recall what was here
by the time spring rolled around.

Don had found some mercury in one of the old cabins. Mercury
has the property of attracting and collecting gold. We knew that the

...rs – and maybe even today's miners – used it to separate collect their fine gold from the black sand. Don had collected a panful of a mixture of black sand and fine gold pieces not quite big enough to pick up with tweezers. He knew the fundamentals of using mercury, but had never actually put them to use. Now, with a little time on his hands, he decided to give this method a try.

I am always nervous, and therefore cautious about trying new things. I envisioned us losing our teeth, hair or some other required body part. The old miners had told of such happenings, so I didn't want Don to do it. He finally persuaded me by assuring that he would take every necessary precaution.

We lit a fire outdoors. Then both Don and I put on rubber gloves. We made sure that we were facing away from any breeze that might carry the fumes toward us. Protected as if we were going on a space mission, we proceeded to use the mercury.

I'm not sure what rays, fumes or form of attack I envisioned would "jump" out if all these precautions weren't taken. My imagination under circumstances like these can run pretty wild, though, so I wasn't going to take any chances.

I supervised the entire operation, even though I knew nothing about it, and gave Don lots of "advice" regarding what to do in this unknown experiment. Don, and others that know me, have come to believe that the name "Gwen" must be synonymous with sterilising, bleaching and anything else that keeps things germ-free.

We ended up with a blob of gold that weighed approximately two and a half ounces!

True to my character, I had Don burn everything that had touched the mercury. On completion of the experiment, I bleached my hands and then gave them a good wash. It probably didn't do any good, but it seemed the thing to do. Then I insisted that the mercury-treated gold should not touch any of the other gold. God forbid it should contaminate any of the other gold! At my insistence, Don put this gold in a separate glass container in the cookhouse – well-sealed, you may be sure!

The tale doesn't end here. Later in the week, during our hasty leave-taking of Barker Creek, that jar of gold got left right there in the cookhouse. It wasn't missed until we were in the Dawson mining recording office.

180

We put all of the camp supplies into large plastic garbage barrels with lids. This was to prevent any mice nesting in, or running through, our things during our camp vacancy. We had chosen to leave all of our clothing except what we required for the trip home. We were also leaving all the bedding, new sheets and a hefty supply of towels. These had been brought for our company – remember all the guests we'd expected during the summer?

In the spring, Don had brought a supply of pants, including some new ones, which were as yet unused. He had actually managed to get through the entire season wearing the old ones. This supply of pants was also left in one of the garbage barrels. We did decide to take two sleeping bags for use when we stopped over at our Dease Lake cabin on the way home. We cleaned out the fridge and freezer, and then we were set to go.

Don had already phoned Trans North and told them that we could be ready within an hour's notice for the next available helicopter. Dawson's weather had been quite foggy of late, making flying uncertain. We had our radiophone in operation to receive any messages regarding our flight out. One load of goods already awaited us in Dawson. We had sent it a few days ago. We were hoping that we'd be able to follow in a few days, but as it stood now, the helicopter couldn't come. After the kind of life we'd been leading, can you imagine what it felt like to have time on our hands, to be looking for something to do? It was almost unheard of. We fixed that in a hurry!

I remembered the cocoa matting we had taken out of the sluicebox when we'd exchanged it for the new, sophisticated sluice-box carpeting. I suggested we try to retrieve any gold that might have caught in it. It sounded like a great idea. I just wasn't sure how to go about it. The matting was wet and heavy. Neither of us can remember whose idea it was to burn the carpet. Whoever thought of it had the idea that the ashes would be panned.

The problem was that the cocoa matting refused to burn. Neither of us will admit to whose idea it was to put used machine oil in the fire to get it to burn. It matters not, because it didn't work either. Nothing did. "That sure doesn't want to burn," said a frustrated Don.

"Well, pour more oil on it," I said, refusing to give up. We eventually came to the conclusion that this matting was not, no matter how much we wanted it to, going to burn.

We've often spoken of this incident with a great deal of unresolved curiosity. What did that mat hold? Could it have been a small fortune in fine gold? To this day, the answer to that lies with the mat, buried under the following year's mining, and claimed forevermore by the Barker ground.

Finally accepting defeat by the mysterious nonflammable mat, Don and I set off for bed on our last night at camp. By morning the weather had improved, so we were quite sure that the chopper would no longer be delayed. I kept out some emergency food items and made a batch of sandwiches. This would suffice until we reached Dawson. Again, we left a supply of dried foods and other essentials in an unlocked cabin, in case anyone came by and was in need during our absence.

To make certain that everything was ready for next spring, and because we needed something else to do with our time, we double-checked all items. At 4 p.m. we finally received a radio message that a large 204B helicopter would be coming for us that evening. It arrived, as promised, around 8 p.m. It was almost dusk by the time we'd finished loading up our gear. We jumped into the chopper and were Dawson bound.

From the air, we took a last look at the camp. We were satisfied that everything was in shape for the long winter, and the following spring. I didn't know at the time that I was seeing the Barker Creek camp and our gold claims for the last time.

Our pilot was Doug Makkonen, someone we had flown with before. Soon after we were airborne the three of us heard a strange vibrating noise. It wasn't only the pilot that knew this was not a usual helicopter sound. He got out his flying manual, and quickly flipped pages. We assumed he was trying to pinpoint the problem. Usually quite talkative, he was now preoccupied and silent. Don and I were pretty quiet ourselves. I think we all had a lot of concerns going through our minds.

Though we knew that the pilot had taken the shortest route possible, that flight seemed like the longest one we'd ever taken to Dawson. A massive sigh of relief was expelled by all when we finally had our feet firmly planted on Dawson City soil. Later we

Don at beginning of season and Don at end of season
—what a difference a summer makes!

learned that the helicopter had suffered a cracked frame. It did not fly again until the following spring. The helicopters get regular scheduled maintenance, but it just proves that anything can go wrong, at any time.

By the time we arrived in Dawson City, all of the eating places were closed for the night and we were only able to get a sandwich in a bar. Many of the hotels had closed after Labour Day weekend, but knowing this ahead of time, we'd reserved one. We were looking forward to a leisurely hot shower and shampoo after the months of our Yukon shower. We were terribly disappointed to find that the water in the taps was almost cold.

The following morning, our first job was to take our gold to the Dawson mining office, have it recorded, pay the royalty and have a seal put on the container. Dave Jennings was surprised with the size of our big nugget. Beams of delight spread across our faces when it tipped the scale at eight and a half ounces. It is believed to be the largest found in the area in 1981. There were rumours of a 30-ounce nugget, but many believe this nugget grew in the bars after a few rounds of drinks. Dave recorded our big nugget separately from the balance of our gold.

After tying up the last of the loose ends and settling all our accounts, we headed down the Klondike Highway to our next stop – Pelly Ranch. After leaving the highway, it took us an hour and a half to get there. Dick and Marjorie made us feel very welcome. Marjorie told us we'd have to stay for supper, and overnight. We gratefully conceded to her wishes.

Don renewed his acquaintance with Dick's brother, Hugh, and I met him for the first time. The farm is in a beautiful setting; the river flows right by it. Stooks of golden-yellow oats stood out in the field.

On the way home we made stops at Watson Lake, Dease Lake, Vanderhoof and Salmon Arm. In Salmon Arm, we stopped at Don's mother's. Mom Lee was watering plants in her garden as our truck pulled up in her yard. It was amusing to see Don's mother squinting at him, unable to believe it was Don. She'd never seen him with long hair and sporting a beard. He promised he'd have his hair cut once he got home. He looked like a true sourdough prospector. She recognized me right away, but didn't know her own son!

During the last few days of our trek home to Langley, the temperature had been a warm 80°F. Don said that with the weather so sunny and bright, he almost felt like he'd quit too soon, and was playing hooky.

CHAPTER 24

Losing Big Time – Adios to Mining

Once home, and finally having the privacy of land-line phones, Don decided to contact Herman about the payment. Once again, Herman said he was unable to make the payment just yet; he promised that it would be coming as soon as he was able. We were beginning to get suspicious, believing that we might never see this happen. In fact, we never did. We don't think he ever intended to pay. It was a heartbreaking lesson for us, and the lessons weren't over yet.

The date eventually rolled around when Herman was legally obligated to have the year's work on Scroggie Creek claims recorded in the Dawson mining office. Payment for recording the work had to be made also. When we didn't receive notification that this had been done, Don phoned the mining office.

To his horror, he found out that Herman had neither recorded any work, nor paid any bills in the Yukon. Unbeknown to us, multiple liens had been registered against the property by suppliers of the services and goods that Herman had not paid for. In the original contract it was stated that the mining claims would revert to Lee's Jade and Opals Ltd.'s name if Herman reneged on paying. Claims were to have full assessment work done and registered, and claims were to be left debt-free. The only part of the contract that was fulfilled was that the claims reverted to the name of Lee's Jade and Opals Ltd.

With the return of the claims to us came all of the liens that Herman's creditors had slapped against the property. These liens totalled approximately $350,000! Unbeknown to us, some of the liens had commenced as early as August 1981. Most of them were in Herman's name, but some were joint liens with Ahlamax Mines Ltd., Herman's mining company.

We could hardly believe what we were hearing, but black-and-white printed reports soon reached us by mail, in which we could see that the return of the claims from Herman to Lee's Jade and Opals Ltd. was officially recorded. The document bears the stamp, "December 10, 1981, Mining Recorder, Dawson, Y.T." This transfer of claims also transferred all the liens to us, because the liens were against the property.

Striving to at least hold on to the property, and buy time to tackle the liens, Don gathered a skeleton crew together. He had to return with these workers to the Yukon in order to do the compulsory assessment work, file it and then return home. (He managed to pick up the sealed jar we had forgotten containing the two and a half ounces of gold processed using mercury.) The next step we took was to seek legal advice.

We were told to meet with the creditors and try to arrive at a percentage on the dollar that would be acceptable to all parties. Once we established a figure, we would need to seek a buyer that was prepared to pay this amount to the creditors. The purchasers would take over and then work the ground. After all the debts were settled, we would be paid our share. This certainly seemed like a workable solution. Well, if there was a law more drastic than Murphy's, we'd found it!

Instead of receiving the money due to us, we ended up putting out another $30,000 for legal and other expenses. The one bright spot in this whole horrendous affair was the White Pass Petroleum company.

White Pass, one of the creditors, deserves to be recognized and thanked for their support in this endeavour. In phone conversations with us, they offered their services in holding meetings with the other creditors until an acceptable percentage was reached. White Pass stated, "We know all the creditors. We know this is not your personal debt, and we wish to help you resolve this."

We gratefully accepted their offer. After the meetings were held and all the creditors had arrived at a figure, it was relayed to us. We then advertised, and found a purchaser who was interested in taking over the property with the outlined terms. Next came the final blow against our keeping Scroggie.

Finning Tractor, the major creditor, had its lawyer write a letter saying that their client was withdrawing from the group decision. They wanted a judicial sale. Consequently, neither we nor the rest of the lien holders ever got any payment. It had become an impossible situation. In the end, we lost the Scroggie Creek claims.

Everyone that we had befriended in the North knew of our plight. They also knew that we had always paid all of the bills we'd incurred. To have such a catastrophe fall on us was devastating. No tears would ever heal this wound. The people of the North are generous and under-standing, and willingly extend credit. This can lead to being taken advantage of – as in this incident – but the debtor's name is quickly spread around the Yukon. In this case, Herman's.

We, however, have been able to hold our heads high, and today we are able to obtain credit anywhere in the Yukon. This we proved several years later when we returned to the Yukon to undertake another commercial venture. When we required letters of recommendation, these same firms readily gave them to us. Thank you, Yukoners.

How did we do with gold mining in this year that had quickly become tumultuous? We were able to pay all of our bills for 1981 and still have some gold left over. Don and I decided that we should have our accountant reduce our equity in Lee's Jade and Opals Ltd. by the value of ten ounces of gold each. We put the 20 ounces of gold in a safety-deposit box – the eight-and-a-half-ounce nugget included. This would be our rainy-day stake, or perhaps a trip at some time.

Unfortunately, we've lost money holding onto the gold, because eighteen years later, we are still working and waiting to take that special trip! Gold prices are lower now than they were then. The feeling of security, though, in knowing that 20 ounces of gold will always be worth something, is rewarding.

We had settled into our Lee's Jade and Opals shop routine quite quickly when we got back from Barker. We began to have family discussions about mining. We were trying to decide among a variety of options. Should we be selling, taking in a partner – or finding another solution altogether? We had faith in the property, but we knew that we couldn't cope the way things stood.

More gravel would have to be put through the sluice each day to make it profitable. Also, the equipment would have to be worked for longer hours to warrant the monthly leasing cost. Something called a live sluice-box should be used. This is a vibrating, shaking system that screens and prevents large rocks from going into the actual box. It's a method that uses less water and allows only smaller rocks in the sluice-box run, preventing rock jams and loss of gold. The cost and time involved in all these things was beginning to seem like too much.

Finally, the word was out that we anticipated either selling or leasing the property. A cash offer came in that was extremely tempting – until we spoke to our accountant. He told us the amount of income tax we would have to pay, and we quickly turned down the offer. We then began looking for someone interested in a lease-to-purchase arrangement. We felt it would also be necessary to sell our equity in the equipment and arrange for the machinery leases with Finning to be transferred to any new owner's name. This would guarantee that we wouldn't get any large repair bills, or be responsible if the equipment wasn't looked after or payments weren't made. In order to do this, however, we would have to part with our equity at a loss.

In retrospect, we wish that we'd taken that cash offer, paid the taxes and enjoyed the balance of the money. It was far more difficult to find parties interested in gold property that year, because the gold price had dropped. It had been US$800 per ounce the previous year – a record high. By December of 1981, it had dropped to about US$550. When the 1982 mining season commenced, there was another $100 drop. The gold price remained quite constant throughout the entire mining season. Many of the gold-mining operations had been expecting a price increase before the season ended, but it never happened.

Early in 1982, an established mining company listed on the Toronto Stock Exchange,Queenstake Mining, expressed an interest in our property. Between us, we drew up a workable contract. Forrest and a helper made the winter trip in, and Queenstake worked the property for that year. Everything went according to the contract, but that season was not a good one for mining.

When Don and I had left Barker, we fully expected we'd be making a return trip in the spring of 1982. When it became apparent that this would no longer occur, we began thinking about the many items that we wished to recover from Barker. These included such things as the Suzuki motorcycle, our sleeping bags and bedding, and that supply of Don's pants that we'd left.

We were given a promise by Queenstake that these articles would be brought to Dawson by helicopter. From there, we would make arrangements to transport them to Langley. Well, the season was quickly passing, but no goods were being flown out. Several phone calls later, we finally got the news that our items awaited us in Whitehorse.

Don and I made the trip to Whitehorse to collect them. What we found there were a couple of boxes and garbage bags full of everything but what we'd expected. For instance, there were dirty, used work pants. They were at least a 48-inch waist – Don's is 34 inches. One thing came that I recognized – my work boots. It's a fair guess that I would have gotten them, because no one working at Barker could have put them on their feet. To this day I have them. I look at them and reminisce about the times when they were worn, the many miles they covered while on my feet.

Next Queenstake, with our permission, sold the contract for working Barker claims. Two Wright brothers bought it. No, these were not the Wrights connected with the first airplanes, although they did own one. These Wrights were from Nevada. Don and I met them and went over the contract with them. They agreed to begin work the following spring, and in June of 1984 we signed the contract with Dave and Gayland Wright.

The time arrived for them to start mining. We know that they did go into Barker, but the season was swiftly passing by, and no mining was getting done. They claimed to be having trouble acquiring both help and equipment. We finally told them we'd forget any payment that year, and instead begin working, as per the contract, the following year. Don and I didn't really have much choice, as the price of gold had dropped again. We learned that several other properties in the Dawson mining area had been in financial difficulty. They'd been taken over at a bankruptcy rate. For us, this meant that there were no people standing in line to deal on our property.

Another year rolled by and still no payments came from the

Wrights. Dave Wright was on Barker Creek. He gave us a multitude of excuses as to why they hadn't paid us yet. Then he returned to Nevada. Don made many phone calls to Dave, who continued to say that he was working out a payment method. It began to sound familiar.

He also told us that he'd found a purchaser for the property. He gave Don many details, and it sounded sincere. In fact, Don fully believed him. We were elated that we were going to have a cash buyer. Dave told us that the delay was because his lawyer wouldn't do any further work for him unless Dave paid him US$1200. We were so completely convinced that it meant a sale, that we wired Dave the $1200. With the exchange, it was over $1700 Canadian.

Soon after this, we received a letter from the U.S. court, stating that Dave Wright had filed for bankruptcy. We were listed as a creditor, but wouldn't be seeing one cent of the money owed to us – there was none. That ended the episode between the Wrights and the Lees.

What more could happen? Well, there was still one more blow to come. White Pass had placed a $12,000 lien against the property because of the Wrights' unpaid bills. We had to settle this immediately or it would be impossible to negotiate any interest in, or sale of, the property. It was devastating, but we somehow managed to pay it.

By now we were physically, mentally and financially at the end of our rope. We had our land back, but no manpower, no equipment to do work and no money to buy these things. There was no way we could commence mining, and our options were narrowing. We were no longer sure that there was a way to hang on to the Barker property, either.

During this time a disruption occurred in our close family. Linda and Forrest had decided to separate. This is always a difficult experience for a family to go through. Needless to say, it was a traumatic year.

In the end, we were able to hold on to the Barker Creek property for two more years. The assessment work was done, and this gave us a grace period during this time, whether or not any mining work was done.

Meanwhile, in 1986, the Expo 86 world's fair was being held in Vancouver, B.C., 40 miles west of Langley. What an exciting time that was! Don and I went to Expo and organized a number of meetings in Vancouver at the same time, as several parties had expressed an interest in leasing or purchasing the claims on Barker. On some Tuesdays – our regular day off from the shop – we attended two meetings before heading for Expo.

These expeditions temporarily eased our worries. It was a joy to find nations from all corners of the world existing in peace with one another, sharing their technology, customs and cultures on this small site in B.C. Don and I spent many happy hours experiencing the sights, sounds and unique rhythms of the numerous pavilions.

Throughout the summer and on into the fall, we continued to hold many meetings, but it was impossible to obtain a final commitment from any party to aid in the Barker mining. Deals would get all but finalized, only to collapse at the last minute. The low gold price endured, and this did not help in the negotiations.

On one occasion a gentleman representing a mining consortium requested a sample of the gold nuggets that we'd mined on the property. He wanted them to be left with him, in order for his group to see the various sizes and quality. Don and I were so anxious to make a deal that we took a jar of 18 ounces of nuggets, and put it in the hands of this man.

A week later we arrived at the appointment to collect the nuggets. Fortunately, the contents of the jar were the same as when we'd handed it over. We were told that there was a keen interest in the property. Don and I found the terms unsuitable, however, and we closed the negotiations.

Days, weeks, months and then finally two years went by. Truly, time waits for no man.

On Thanksgiving weekend in 1988 another upsetting incident occurred in our close family – our son Brian and his wife, Cathy, told us that they had decided to have a trial separation. This subsequently led to a divorce. However, it was an amicable separation and both of them remained in the same district, so we still had the ties with our grandchildren.

Meanwhile, we were feeling desperate and pursuing any avenue that might help us hold on to our claims. When a man named Larry Bratvold contacted us, we thought that he could be the answer to our prayers. He also owned claims on Barker, and had found an interested party who was proposing to lease or purchase both of our claims. We knew our options had nearly run dry, so we listened keenly to this one.

Larry had done some testing on his ground and had obtained results similar to ours. We had some large nuggets, pictures and records to support the information we gave. There were several meetings, discussing all the details, and then each party met with their respective lawyer to draft a contract for negotiating purposes.

The new backers would mine both claims and would be listed on the Vancouver Stock Exchange (VSE). We felt comfortable entering this agreement, whereby we'd receive an initial down payment of $50,000. We also had a guaranteed yearly payment based on production. A provision was made that we would receive a penalty payment if no mining was done in a single year. In the contract, we were given permission to visit and view the property any time we chose. We never did exercise that privilege. Had we done so, it may have changed, delayed or maybe even prevented some of the problems that arose.

The mining was carried out under the name Havilah Gold Mines Ltd. We were to have no involvement in the mining. We were offered shares at 50 cents per share, prior to them being listed on the Vancouver Stock Exchange. It was estimated that they'd have a value of approximately $1.00 per share, once listed. Having faith in the Barker property, we decided to invest our total down payment in the purchase of shares. For a short while the shares were on the market for the expected $1.00 share value. They dropped, but we purchased more. We believed that we had "inside knowledge." Don and I and other family members ended up spending in excess of $80,000 to secure shares.

The first year of operation ended, and it was time for us to receive the money due as the yearly payment. It arrived late, but none of us experienced any depth of concern. We anticipated that everything would become streamlined the following year. Looking back, we now realize that we should have insisted that everything be carried out as per the contract. This would have spared us a future disaster.

With Havilah in control of all operations on the property, mining continued to limp along the following year. At this season's end the payment was tardy once again, but eventually made. We had some concern at this point. The value of our shares on the VSE was declining – down to 10 cents each. We purchased even more, though, thinking that it would equalize the overall cost of our shares, and planned to sell them when we could recover our money. By this time it was becoming obvious that the mining was not being done to our expectations.

Don had designed some mining equipment. It was for use in testing various types of ground. It consisted of a three-inch pump, hose and live sluice-box. Larry and associates felt this would be invaluable for further testing on Barker. Havilah arranged to purchase it from Lee's Jade and Opals. The majority of the negotiated price was paid to us, but a small amount continued to show in unpaid accounts.

For the 1991 year, we didn't receive any payment from Havilah. Limited correspondence came from Gold Leaf Management Ltd., where Larry Bratvold was a director. Communication with Havilah was becoming difficult. Our phone calls and faxes were going unanswered. The New Era Development shares were down to 2 cents per share. Don and I sensed something was very wrong. It was now useless to attempt to sell any shares. We held all we had purchased, and they finally became worthless. They were eventually delisted from the VSE.

In March 1992, Larry Bratvold and Ronald Campbell, both directors of Gold Leaf Management Ltd., visited us. They explained that they'd had financial problems, but with our cooperation, felt that they could overcome the situation. A group of investors was willing to put up money to mine Havilah/Gold Leaf Management gold properties, which included Barker, in the 1992 mining season. They surprised Don and me with an unexpected proposal. They requested that we arrive at a figure we would accept as a one-time, final payment for all of our interest in the mining property. Larry and Ronald told us that the investors would be happier if Gold Leaf Management was the sole owner.

This made sense to Don and me. We reasoned that if we offered it for a low price, we should be able to get a quick settlement, and have some money in our hands. We certainly weren't getting anything the way things were going; this sounded like our best option.

After deliberating, we said we'd accept $62,500 – a mere $12,500 over what was already owed to us. It was a giveaway, fire-sale price, but the constant problems and worries were taking their toll on us. I'd recently undergone surgery for breast cancer, so more worries were the last thing we needed then.

The quoted sum was satisfactory to Larry and Ronald. Payment in full was to be made to us by June 1, 1992. This date rolled around but no cheque arrived. We made many phone calls to Larry, but none were returned. All of the efforts we took to secure payment were to no avail.

Bad news was followed by more bad news. All the turmoil and frustrations of 1992 and 1993 were capped when, through a fluke, we learned that we were no longer the owners of any claims on Barker Creek! It had been in the contract that Havilah, now Gold Leaf Management, record, and pay the recording fee for, the assessment work done on Barker. This had apparently been done – however, the cheque was returned N.S.F. and the error was not corrected within the permitted grace period. This allowed the Barker Creek claims to become open ground in the Dawson Mining District. It was available to anyone who wished to stake and record the claims as their own. Someone had.

Had Don and I known of the N.S.F. cheque, we would have done something to ensure continued possession of the property. It was now too late to do anything to have the claims restored to us. Just like that, our ownership ceased. The two of us were crushed by this turn of events. I was feeling especially bitter to think that we'd once again lost our mining property.

New Era Developments Ltd., or as it was later called, Gold Leaf Management Ltd., was "dissolved/removed" by the VSE on August 20, 1993 for failure to file the mandatory annual report. This information we found later in the Corporate Registry, Province of B.C.

One day a phone call came for Don. The disturbing content of that call was like rubbing salt in an open wound. A man's voice at the other end asked, "Do you want to buy some claims on Barker Creek?"

"Hell, no!" shouted Don, "I'm supposed to own them!" He hung up the phone. This man had staked and recorded the claims when they'd become open ground after the N.S.F. cheque fiasco.

Shortly after this incident, we learned that some of the investors who had put up money to mine Havilah Gold Mines/New Era

Developments/Gold Leaf Management claims, which included the Barker Creek claims, were starting a class-action suit to sue for the loss of their investment. It was rumoured that over $2 million had been raised and very little mining had been done. Don and I really wanted to join this class action. We made an appointment with the lawyer.

After explaining our position to him, the lawyer offered us his sympathy. Regretfully, he told us, we couldn't be a party to it, because our interest was in the land itself, but the investors' claim was regarding investment on the land – the two could not be grouped. He would have to treat us as a separate case. We declined, explaining that we had no more good money to throw after bad. When we walked out of his office, we closed the door on another epoch of our mining days.

Havilah Gold Mines Ltd. was dissolved by the VSE on January 14, 1994 – also for failure to file. This information, gleaned from the Corporate Registry, Province of B.C., somehow did not come as a surprise to Don and me. . . .

We may not have mining claims in the Yukon any more, but we are still very much a part of the respected community in the North. The friends and acquaintances that we made during our years there continue to value the experiences and memories we share with them.

In the summer of 1998 Al Kapty, the owner of Trans North Helicopters, stopped in at our gift shop in Dawson to talk to me. We reminisced about our last frightening helicopter ride from Barker Creek. He recollected that the Bell 204 had experienced a cracked frame, and confirmed that it had taken most of the winter to rebuild that helicopter. Al told me that Doug Makkonen – the pilot for that ride – was still with them. After all these years, Al readily remembered the incident.

Although there were a number of times in our mining days that we were not treated according to the Golden Rule, on more than one occasion Don has asserted, "We have never inflicted an injustice on anyone, and we will not be bitter, but get on with our lives." He has been my pillar of strength through the many ordeals that we've faced.

In spite of everything, the Yukon mining saga gave the Lee family the satisfaction of taking a piece of wilderness and developing it into a producing gold mine. We did not get rich, if monetary returns were the single measure. We realize we were lucky, though. We actually fared better than many who venture into the financial abyss of Yukon mining. The years that we were in full control of the property, we extracted sufficient gold to pay all of our bills. We even showed some profit, allowing us to expand the mining venture the following year. For a small crew, the work that was accomplished was monumental. The winter overland trips were truly epics of achievement.

Learning life's lessons along the way, we lived an adventure that most people only dream or read about. Although no pot of gold magically appeared at the end of the Lee rainbow, we gained immeasurable experience, unforgettable memories and lasting friendships.

Afterword 2000

The adventuresome nature of the Lee family keeps them constantly moving into new endeavours. They do this while maintaining ties with people throughout B.C. and the Yukon.

Today Don and Gwen Lee call themselves semi-retired. They continue to own and operate Lee's Jade and Opals Ltd. in Langley, B.C. In Dawson City, Rivers of Gold Gifts is another family owned and operated business, presently managed by Gwen.

Brian and his wife, Sally, a notary public, reside in Abbotsford, B.C., 20 miles east of Langley. Brian is the owner of Lee's Fine Jewellery Ltd.

Linda and her husband, Scott, own and operate the Northern Beaver Post and the Wolf It Down Restaurant. These are located side by side at Mile 650 of the Alaska Highway in the Yukon, half a mile from the junction of Highway 37 and the Alaska Highway. Linda and Scott have two daughters: Amber, twelve, and Kelsey, ten.

On land adjoining the Wolf It Down Restaurant, the family is developing The Baby Nugget RV Park.

Epilogue 2004

Nugget City is on the map! The Lee and Goodwin interest in the Yukon continues to expand. The Northern Beaver Post, Wolf It Down Restaurant, Cabins, and Baby Nugget RV Park comprise a new city situated at historic mile 650 of the Alaska Highway. A gas-diesel bar and repair shop will be added in 2004. Continuing development plans for the future include a tire shop and a tenting area.

Lee's Jade and Opals Ltd. has been closed and now Don and Gwen's business interests are strickly personal in the Yukon. Are they retiring? You guess!

Don and Gwen on their fiftieth wedding
anniversary, Oct. 31/1998.

The Lee family's Rivers of Gold Gifts in Dawson City.

Carved door at The Northern Beaver Post in Nugget City, Yukon. Carved by Roger Latondre

The Northern Beaver Post and Wolf It Down Restaurant at Mile 650, Alaska Highway, owne and operated by Linda and Scott.

Aerial view of Nugget City, Mile 650, Alaska Highway 2003.

The Northern Beaver Post store, restaurant and RV park at Beaver Post, Yukon.

RCMP in ceremonial dress at a Beaver Post fundraiser for a sick child.

Glossary

ALLUVIAL SOIL • sand, mud and earth left by flowing water

BEDROCK • solid rock beneath the alluvial material

BENCH • a fairly level stretch of ground that runs higher than, and parallel to, the valley bottom

BLACK SAND • heavy particles, black in colour, that are resistant to separation from fine gold

CATCH BASIN • a large hole dug in the earth to collect the water after sluicing and hold it until it is clear enough to be put back into the creek; also called a settling pond

CHECHAKO • a greenhorn; the name given to newcomers arriving in the Yukon in 1898

CINNAMON BUN STRIP • nickname used for Brayeburn, a stop on the Klondike Highway

CLEAN-UP • the process of washing the cocoa mat or other carpet to retrieve gold after sluicing

COARSE GOLD • refers to larger-size nuggets

COCOA MAT • a rough-textured mat placed in the bottom of the sluice box to catch the gold as the gravel is washed through

CRIBBING • the wooden lining inside a mine shaft that prevents it from caving in

CUTTING A (CENTRE) LINE • making a trail through the brush and marking it with ribbons to mark off a leased area; in placer mining, since all leases have a fixed width set by the government, only a centre line is required

DEISTER TABLE • a mechanized table that separates materials according to weight

DREDGE • a small dredge is a suction machine used in testing; it sucks up soil, gravel and gold from beneath the water. Large dredges have a chain-and-bucket system to bring material to the surface for processing and then gold retrieval

FINENESS • percentage of pure gold when assayed; the Barker claims consistently tested 89 percent pure gold, 9 percent silver and 2 percent impurities–among the highest fineness in the Yukon

FOUR-BY-FOUR • a four-wheel-drive vehicle

GEARMATIC WINCH • hydraulic-powered drum with cable

GOLD SPINNER • a small centrifuge used to separate gold and black sand

GUNNY SACK • burlap bag

HALE PUMP • a brand of water pump powered by a Perkins diesel motor. Ours had a five-inch suction, a four-inch discharge and would pump 1200 gallons per minute

HYDRAULICING • process of using high-pressure water to erode and remove overburden and muck

ICE LUGS • extra steel cleats welded onto steel bulldozer treads to provide traction on ice

IN SITU • material found in its original place

JILLPOKE • stick into; jab or poke, as in small trees poking their way into machinery

LAPIDARY • having to do with cutting or engraving precious stones to make jewellery, carvings, etc.

LOWBED • a low trailer on wheels that when connected to a truck is used to haul heavy equipment such as bulldozers

LOADER BUCKET • front scoop on a piece of equipment such as a tractor or loader

MINING TAGS • tags that get fastened to 4" x 4" stakes driven into the ground in a line to mark off a claim. They contain the date of staking the claim, the owner's name, etc.

MUSKEG • swamp or marsh covered with moss or other vegetation

NEOPHYTES • beginners

OVERBURDEN • vegetation, soil and muck above gold-bearing gravel

PANNING • old-fashioned way of washing gravel in a hand-held pan, now mainly used for testing ground value

PENNYWEIGHT SCALE • scale to measure small quantities of gems or precious metals; a pennyweight equals 24 grains or 1/20 of an ounce. *See* TROY

PERMAFROST • ground or subsoil found in the North that is permanently frozen

PLACER MINING • the process of washing loose sand or gravel for gold or other minerals

RIFFLES • stepped ridges in the sluice-box

RIPPER • one or two big teeth mounted vertically at the rear of a bulldozer, used for breaking up earth

ROCKHOUNDING • the hobby of collecting rocks

SETTLING POND • same as a catch basin

SCHIST • fairly soft, layered rock formation; shale

SKIFF OF SNOW • a light snowfall

SLUICE-BOX • in placer mining, a long sluice fitted with riffles, in which gold-bearing gravel is washed and the gold is separated from the gravel, muck, etc.

SOURDOUGH • a seasoned resident; in Gold Rush days, someone who had spent at least one winter in the Yukon

STRIPPING • removing the overburden to expose gold-bearing gravel

TROY, or TROY WEIGHT • a system of weights used for precious metals and gemstones, based on the grain. 24 grains=1 pennyweight; 20 pennyweights=1 (troy) ounce; 12 ounces=1 (troy) pound. Named after the city of Troyes, France, where it was first used

WINCH • a power-driven machine for lifting or pulling

WINCH LINE • the cable on the winch

WIND SOCK • cone-shaped sleeve mounted on a pole that indicates wind direction for pilots

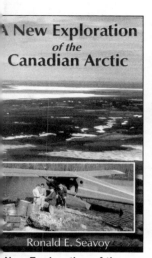

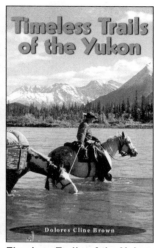

New Exploration of the
Canadian Arctic
Ronald E. Seavoy
ISBN 0-88839-522-1
5.5 x 8.5 • sc • 192 pp.

Gem Trails of
British Columbia
Cam Bacon
ISBN 0-88839-498-5
5.5 x 8.5 • sc • 96 pp.

Timeless Trails of the Yukon
Dolores Cline Brown
ISBN 0-88839-484-5
5.5 x 8.5 • sc • 184 pp.

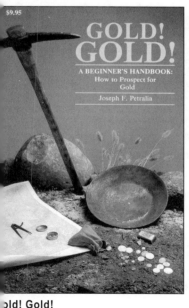

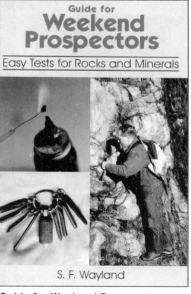

Gold! Gold!
Joseph F. Petralia
ISBN 0-88839-118-8
5.5 x 8.5 • sc • 110 pp.

Guide for Weekend Prospectors
S. F. Wayland
ISBN 0-88839-405-5
5.5 x 8.5 • sc • 96 pp.

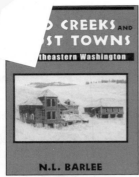

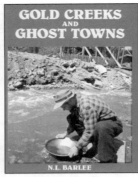

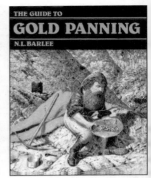

**Gold Creeks and Ghost
Towns of Northeastern
Washington**
N.L. Barlee
ISBN 0-88839-452-7
8.5 x 11 • sc • 224 pp.

**Gold Creeks and Ghost
Towns (BC)**
N. L. Barlee
ISBN 0-88839-988-X
8.5 x 11 • sc • 192 pp.

**The Guide to Gold
Panning**
N. L. Barlee
ISBN 0-88839-986-3
8.5 x 11 • sc • 192 pp.

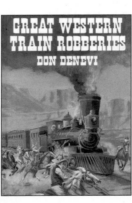

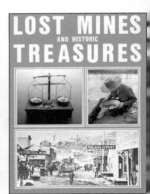

**Buckskins, Blades and
Biscuits**
Allen Johnston
ISBN 0-88839-363-6
5.5 x 8.5 • sc • 176 pp.

**Great Western Train
Robberies**
Don DeNevi
ISBN 0-88839-287-7
5.5 x 8.5 • sc • 208 pp.

**Lost Mines and Historic
Treasures**
N. L. Barlee
ISBN 0-88839-992-8
8.5 x 11• sc • 96 pp.

View all HANCOCK HOUSE
titles at
www.hancockhouse.com

HANCOCK HOUSE PUBLISHERS
1431 Harrison Avenue, Blaine, WA 98230-5005
www.hancockhouse.com